GROW

12 UNCONVENTIONAL LESSONS FOR BECOMING AN UNSTOPPABLE ENTREPRENEUR

GROW

MIKE FATA

PAGE TWO

Cataloguing in publication information is available from Library and Archives Canada.
ISBN 978-1-77458-341-8 (paperback)
ISBN 978-1-77458-342-5 (ebook)

Page Two
pagetwo.com

Edited by James Harbeck
Copyedited by Steph VanderMeulen
Proofread by Alison Strobel
Cover design by Peter Cocking
Interior design by Setareh Ashrafologhalai
and Peter Cocking
Illustrations by Setareh Ashrafologhalai

mikefata.ca

*To the best mentor I've
ever had: my mom, Debbie.*

CONTENTS

INTRODUCTION
WHAT HAPPENS NEXT, NOW

I'VE ALWAYS liked trying to figure out what might happen next. I used to geek out reading multi-ending storybooks when I was a kid. I loved reading and reading, trying all the different options to see what endings I could reach. I liked scenario planning and destination exploration, following the clues on each page to challenge myself, trying to predict what might happen if I made different choices.

Life, though, is not a storybook. We have a choice about what we do with the time we have on Earth. We have a choice in each direction we take. Sometimes it feels as if we are limited to just two or three paths forward, just like in those storybooks. But each of our stories has a million or more pathways to try out.

It's the same in the world of business.

When we start out in business, often we'll just shortcut to our vision and mission statements. We pull our strategies from any business website or university course and add them to our own plan. We do that because we feel like there's a specific checklist we have to follow, with checkboxes created by someone who's been on the path ahead of us. We follow other people's timelines. We get scared and nervous when we follow these so-called rules and we don't get to where we want to go fast enough.

The thing is, other people's paths, rules, and timelines don't mean anything.

All that matters is that you're authentic in showing up for your own life. Once you've got that down, your business outcomes can and will be extraordinary, even if they're unconventional.

I'm a big believer in transparency in business.

Let's start with an open-book accounting, balanced scorecard kind of transparency: Here are the good things happening; here are the bad things happening. Here's where we have to get together and figure out what's next; here's where we can slow down. The more information we have about what's going on, and the more we tackle problems openly as a team, the more likely it is that we're going to be successful.

I'm also a big believer in transparency in life. I have no barriers when it comes to telling you about the different and sometimes painful challenges I have faced that have shaped who I am and how my business emerged from my life experiences. The more we understand about ourselves and each other, the more we're likely to get where we want to be. We can learn through authenticity because it allows us to address the fears, gaps, and barriers we face together.

The reason I've decided to share my life authentically in this book also has a business reason at its core: what is true for business is also true for life, and vice versa.

In fact, because the work we do is *in the world*, no matter what business idea we have, it's always going to be about people. In that way, *not* being authentic is actually a barrier to success.

Why? It comes back to choice again. When we are authentic about what's important to us, no matter what aspect of life we're talking about, we get to actually choose our values. We get to say out loud: "This is my truth, these are the things I care about, and this is what I want to spend time doing."

Back in 1998, I cofounded Manitoba Harvest Hemp Foods. We didn't write a lot of our values down, but we were out there, building our community, and I just started telling people my own personal story, one that began with my life as a three-hundred-pound teenage dropout and ended with a product that I developed to help people based on my own personal health journey. In every conversation I had, that story just naturally came out. I couldn't help but tell it because people wanted to hear it.

Several years later, together with our much bigger team, we did an exercise with a large firm helping us with strategic planning and brand positioning. We started naming what mattered to us: quality, honesty, transparency, integrity, trust, and a can-do attitude. And as we listed these corporate values one by one, several team members just came out and said, "Oh, those are Mike's values." And they were. Having a business grounded in authentic values meant that our business had meaning and that we were still living the same brand meaning years into our work. Our values at Manitoba Harvest weren't aspirational. They defined how we tried to show up every day. Those values represented how we made our choices, and they mattered to us. They mattered to me.

We all need to be ourselves fully before we follow our passion. We need to be unapologetically ourselves. If you aren't true to who you are, it won't be *your* passion that you're following. It will be someone else's.

That's the whole prerequisite for finding the right path: making the choice that works for *you*.

This isn't to say that you can't ever take other people into account. In fact, you have to do even more than that and put other people's needs first when you're leading a team. That's something we're going to piece out later in this book. But without making a choice that works for you, you're going to be disconnected from the work *and* the team you build, right from the first step forward. Think about what that would actually look like in practical terms. Knowing yourself and what you want and need is critical to showing up fully committed, fully intentional, and focused.

The right path *is* the unconventional path.

The experiences and traumas I've had in my life defined me and helped me create my business, so I don't want to shy away from them in this book.

Nor should you shy away from yours.

The world is waking up to the qualities that an unconventional path offers all of us. As businesspeople, or as individuals who want to see themselves grow, we need to be transparent with ourselves and find out who we truly are so that we can pursue the path that actually matters to us. And the path can be winding; that's okay. A straight shot down a highway is never as interesting as a ramble up a mountain.

Even though I built my business big enough to make a nine-figure exit in 2019, I've had to deal with the impact of imposter syndrome at multiple stages of my business career. And yet, I was always under the impression, when I was younger, that I was going to fake it till I made it. But those two feelings collided. I had to admit to myself when I was scared shitless, and when I started to tell others how I felt, I discovered that many of them were in that same space.

I've had team members who have opened up to me, especially if they were being promoted, who felt the same way. People are, by and large, uncomfortable when they get new responsibilities; they worry they might not be able to do the job they've been hired to do. Team members have told me that they felt like they tricked me into believing in them, and as a result, they thought they couldn't do the job they wanted *and* deserved. Every time I heard that, I would remind them that they *weren't* going to be perfect right away, and that they *were going to be* an expert at it soon. They would figure out for themselves how to address their own gaps and grow into a role, and they were allowed to take on that opportunity to grow. They didn't have to feel trapped in imposter syndrome for long. I trusted them.

Really, every step we take is just one moment on our journey. We don't have to hide or be afraid of taking the time we need to get there. And we can create businesses where people feel comfortable enough to share something personal about themselves, because that comfort leads to growth.

As a mentor of new-business founders, however, I know that many people are stuck in their fear of being real, being themselves. Many of us are thinking things like, "I'm going to therapy, but I'm not going to tell anyone that I'm going because they *might* think I have issues." Or "I'm out of shape but I'm not going to tell anyone that I'm going to go to the gym, because I don't want anyone to *think* that I'm out of shape." People think: "If I share this, I'm putting myself at risk." This isn't just true of people at the beginning of their careers, it's everyone.

But the thing that I've learned is that no one gives a shit, because they're worried about their own stuff. And if we all hide these very important pieces about who we are and what we're facing, we might not allow ourselves to leave work early (or on time, even), for example, to actually *go* to therapy and the gym.

Hiding who we are is not going to get us anywhere.

Together, we have to work on the realization that we all need empathy. Leaders especially have to work on this. Everybody's on a journey, and everyone, *every team member in our workplace*, has a journey toward their own growth. As a leader, or as a co-worker, we have to ask ourselves: What's my role in helping them on their growth journey, either through awareness or through support or encouragement?

Here's the thing: as a business and as a society, we deserve better.

We deserve better psychological and physical health at work and at home. And, as someone who works in the natural products space, I also believe that we deserve better when it comes to sustainability. *But all of us have to take the steps to make those ideals real.* We can no longer disconnect our actions in business from who we are as people, and from what we value in our lives. We have to build that alignment, that integrity, that ties all of who we are together.

And so here's the essence of what I'm aiming to share with you in this book. If you can make your own self-led personal changes, and represent your true authentic self in all aspects of your life, you can apply your passions to whatever you want to be doing in business. If you can do that, you're going to be successful.

I believe that because I've seen it over and over again in my work as a founder, and in my work as a mentor. When people like truly being who they are, there's an alignment between who they are and what they do. They find that path where they can create their own spark in a business. Those are the unicorns—the most highly successful businesspeople out there. I think that possibility is within everybody.

On your journey, prime yourself for more magic to happen. Sure, luck happens, but see where the opposite is true.

Having choices can make us feel safe. Choices can delight us. They can allow us to be free to do what we want and be who we are. They can allow us to feel as if we are at play rather than at work. Don't let the world close down around you instead of opening up. Because the funny thing is, we *always* have a choice, even when we don't know we do. Choosing not to grow, for example, would be akin to choosing not to breathe. We can make the choice not to breathe, but the outcome is predictable, and not very positive. Growth is a given and a constant. It's part of who we are. It just is. So knowing that, already, you ought to be able to breathe a bit easier. You know, right now, that you're going to grow and change, no matter what.

The *real choice*, the primary choice that we all make, then, is the choice to resist growth or to embrace it. It is whether or not to have what American psychologist Carol Dweck, author of *Mindset: The New Psychology of Success*, calls a "growth mindset," that ability to look at the world through its opportunities rather than to remain stuck in life's challenges. Either way, we will become something different from what we are right now. There really is no middle ground.

So what path do you want to take?

What direction do you want to go?

Even more important than all of that, what matters to you in how you live your life when you're on that path?

Your choice.

The Easy Ten

Before we go deep, here are ten simple principles to unstop-pable growth that you can start putting into practice right now. They're my core life rules because they work. You may have heard them dozens of times elsewhere, but you may never have taken them to heart before now. You're going to start living by them.

1 Enjoy the journey, there is no destination
2 Be kind to yourself
3 Don't sweat the small stuff
4 Accept that you will never figure everything out
5 Keep forward momentum always
6 Build community daily
7 Give back often and forever
8 Build world-class quality for the win
9 Trust your gut
10 Never sacrifice your health

LESSON 1
A MILLION WINS

F ORTY-TWO YEARS.

That's how long my mom worked as an accountant, every single day of her adult life. That timeline started early, given the fact that she spent most of her time on this planet as a single mom caring for two boys, beginning when I was only two years old. She started out working for a small pharmacy in Thunder Bay, Ontario, which was later bought out by Shoppers Drug Mart, a large national drugstore chain. We moved to Winnipeg when she got offered a role at a bigger store, and she had a long career there. But she also worked several side gigs doing extra accounting work and taking night school classes so that she could get ahead.

She set the stage for me, taught me numbers, and allowed me to become the entrepreneur I am today. She was the truest mentor I ever had because she not only celebrated my successes but also let me fail.

In 2019, she was working for me. For seven years, she had been working full-time for Manitoba Harvest, the company I cofounded in 1998 and had gradually built up over the years. It was only once she was on the team that my mom found herself in a more comfortable financial position, one that finally allowed her some breathing room. She was the first- or second-in-command in finance throughout those years. And when, in September 2018, I decided to sell the company so I could move toward investing in new businesses and helping emerging ideas in the natural health space, she was very supportive, but she was also very clear.

"I'm retiring when I'm sixty-five," she told me.

The problem was that we were right at the beginning of the business deal process. It wouldn't be finalized until February of the new year.

"Finding a replacement for you isn't going to be easy," I said at the time, sitting down with her at brunch with my older brother, Donny.

"Oh, okay. I'll stick on for a couple extra months," she said. "I'll retire the day after the sale closes."

"Mom, what are you gonna do?" Donny asked her.

"I haven't taken more than two weeks off in the forty-two years that I've worked. So the day after I leave work, I'm going to take *three* weeks to decide what I'm going to do." She laughed.

On the last day of those three weeks, my mother passed away.

It was sudden. It was devastating. And it was devastating not only to lose her but also to realize that she had spent every day of her adult life working—and working hard. And then I realized the impact of Mom's life's choices, and it wasn't just that she made ends meet. My mom's choices held spiritual, physical, mental, psychological, and emotional values. My mom's mission was accomplished, so to speak, when she passed. She lived out the portion of her life that she needed to, and then she was released from all her responsibility.

Many times, Mom had said how proud she was to be a single mother who had raised two boys who were successful, who were taking the unconventional way to finding themselves and their purpose.

But the most important thing I learned from her was that no one is special—we *all* have the ability to find success.

You have that ability. You absolutely do.

The trick to following Mom's lesson is that you can't put any barriers in your own way. Not now, not ever. Just because you grow up poor does not mean you can't build wealth. Just because you aren't schooled does not mean you can't be educated. Just because you're unhealthy does not mean you can't build radiant health.

I know this because I've lived it. It wasn't just hard for my mom; it was a difficult life for all of us for a while. When I was eighteen, I was three hundred pounds and I was struggling to find the energy to work and to see my future. Like my mom, I had grown up without a lot of financial or social safety nets. Despite doing well in school, I had dropped out in ninth grade to work in construction. It was the best option in front of me, and I took it.

I am very grateful that I am in the place I am now. I get up in the morning, and I love the life that I'm living. I'm not only here living this experience, but I can live it for another day, and aim for living my best day ever. When I focus on what I want to create in my life for me and my family today rather than what gets in my way, life becomes very fulfilling.

Here's why.

When we decide to start a business or take a vacation or write a book or make any other commitment, we are making the choice to take, let's say, a million steps forward. Each of those steps offers us a chance to take one direction down one path or another, or to make a decision between something that seems to serve us best, and other options that don't make the grade. And, even more, each of those steps offers us a chance to grow—in our field, in our awareness, and in multiple forms of intelligence.

Each of those steps also offers us a chance to take a win and feel good about the step we're on at each moment in the day.

You *can* live **your best day ever, every day.**

Looking at the big picture of our lives, our business decisions, or any of our goals, we all know that success is not a matter of making one solid choice, win or lose, and betting on it. In fact, some of my steps, and your steps, might look like making the best out of a shitty situation and taking a win just for the very fact that we get to sit down at the end of the day and take a deep breath. You can mark off a win if you try out a new habit for an hour—it doesn't have to be for a lifetime. Some wins might be more important to reaching your biggest dream in life, but every win counts. Everything that feels right can be counted as important and can be named as a win. Every step you take also builds on the last. Every time you see yourself do something, you can be proud of yourself for taking a chance on learning, using your skills, and taking a tiny, medium, or large step toward becoming who you want to be.

It's when you add up those million little wins that your life starts to change.

What I've learned more than anything else is that aiming to have those million wins through continuous improvement and constant learning is what matters to success more than any other strategy, plan, or framework.

You *can* live your best day ever, every day.

I'm giving away the ending.

To get to where you want to be, in business or in life, you're going to need to have your best day ever. That's what I want you to understand by the time you reach the end of this book.

What I mean by your *best day ever* is exactly that: feeling good every hour of the day, even while you sleep, because having a best day also allows you to get that all-night sleep you're always missing. And then repeating that best day, not just once, but all the time.

In fact, I recommend that you have your best day ever, every single day, for, give or take, 30,000 consecutive days. Sure, if you really want to get technical about it, you can eliminate the first eighteen years because, let's face it, some of us don't have a lot of choices until we're adults, so we'll whittle that down to 23,430 days. And yes, you're probably not still eighteen right now, so let's average it out at an even 15,000 best days.

Actually, let's not put too much pressure on you. You don't *need* to have your best day ever for 15,000 days.

You *get* to have your best day ever for 15,000 days.

Let's start there.

It may be a common understanding that we are all looking for the answers to what challenges us, but, as the saying goes, the answer to everything we seek in life can be found in the journey itself. I believe that's true, 100 percent. But there's more to your life story than a single journey moving relentlessly forward. Everyone is different, every journey follows a different path, and, when it comes down to it, every decision is unique.

The more important thing to know before we get started is this: our journeys *change us.*

What do the next 15,000 or so days look like for you?

What would you spend time doing if you wanted to have your best day ever?

Who would you want to join you?

Where would you go?

Feel it. Really imagine it out.

That's what business, and life, should feel like.

Having your best day means getting into a space where you feel comfortable enough to be yourself.

Being truly *who you are* means that you're able to fulfill your dream of your own best day ever precisely because you're able to see yourself in that role. This is a really important lesson.

I'll share first. Having my own best day starts and ends with a focus on wellness. Here's what it looks like:

- Seven to eight hours of sleep

- Two to three hours of warming up, stretching, weight training and core exercises, and usually some cardio, ending with more yoga and stretching

- Thermal therapy–like time in a sauna or a hot bath, usually with some breathing exercises and meditation, alternating with cold dips

- Work, both for my portfolio companies and for my own aims, for four to six hours a day

- Mentoring new entrepreneurs in the fields of healthy foods and wellness

- Shopping and cooking for my family, and spending time together

I take my own wellness seriously. It's no joke, but I love taking on the whole plan if I have the time. If I'm on the road or it's a day I'm focusing on my family, I also have an abbreviated version of my plan to fall back on, and that's okay too.

I use my best-day-ever plan not only because it feels good but also because it sets me up for the rest of the day. I'm in my most effective flow state, running in full entrepreneur mode, when my body and mind are relaxed rather than tense. My best-day practice makes me a more consistent and reliable businessperson, father, and partner.

But I can't stress this enough: what works for me is not necessarily going to work for you.
What's important is that you allow yourself to be the center of your own world, to feel good and know your value. You

can check in with yourself and see what's working. It may be that your body needs balance, but there may be other physical, mental, or emotional barriers in your way of having that good-day experience. It's up to you to discover what you need.

For me, for example, anxiety can come up. Before I added a check-in on my emotions as part of my meditation practice, I used to feel that I was on a roller coaster I couldn't control. Now, when I sense myself being jittery or notice I've had no sleep, I know I have the opportunity to turn it around just by paying attention to that feeling. As I've matured with my practice, I've been able to stay in a mindful state for the majority of the day, and that allows me a lot more patience with the people around me as well.

What can you do to take care of your own needs and plan your day around them?

Again, I know there are going to be some short-term roadblocks in your way. I know how hard it is to balance time for work and home commitments. I know all of us go through these cycles in our lives where things are a little bit more challenging.

When I follow my instincts on what I need to feel comfortable and then follow through, I am giving myself a gift. I'm trusting myself.

A successful and fulfilling future is about getting better at making good decisions—the kind of choices we need our imagination to bring into reality. We have to discover and build trust in ourselves so that we become capable and comfortable with everything the world is offering us. We need to trust ourselves in a different way than we have in the past. We need to do this so that we can really get in deep, live our integrity, and make the kind of choices that change what we're expecting from ourselves and others. The same is true for people, companies, and communities: we have to trust our own

This world's not happening to you. **You are happening to the world.**

instincts, and we have to trust those of others, so that we can have more good days.

It took me years of honing my practice to continually have good days, and I'm always resetting my practice depending on my own changing needs. You can take care of your physical, spiritual, and emotional needs by front-loading your self-care at the beginning of the day so you know you're worth your own time, but you can also do it in any way that feels good for you, and that honors who you are.

Even if it's difficult to start, your aim shouldn't be about getting the answers right or wrong. Listen to my mom: none of you is special—every one of you has the ability to find success.

This world's not happening to you. You are happening to the world.

Your million wins are yours to take.

LESSON 2
GIVE BACK EVERY CHANCE YOU GET

AFTER MY parents divorced, I was happy in school and at home. In our new home in Winnipeg, we knew it was going to be a chance to start again.

My brother and I were latchkey kids. Donny was four years older than me, and Mom trusted him to do what needed to be done after school. Most days, after some time playing with our friends, we'd head home and do our chores.

But just a few months before we moved to Winnipeg, I was playing with some older kids, running to catch a ball in a nearby community center playground. I remember looking up at the rapidly moving ball, and I thought I had lined up the catch perfectly. But it just missed my glove and hit me in the head. I don't remember the blood and the ambulance ride, and I woke up in the hospital with a surgical gown on. I had a fractured skull.

The injury shook me up more than a little, and after that reminder of what it felt like to feel fear and pain, I gave up baseball. I started skipping the playground and going straight home. That, and I could see that Mom was working as hard as she could. She was very open and trusting with us because she had to be—otherwise, the three of us wouldn't be able to get by. She treated us like people instead of kids, people who could contribute to our family. It made sense to me to follow her lead. That's why, before I was in my teens, I figured out how to put food on the table, literally.

I liked submarine sandwiches. So I'd go across the street to the grocery shop and get meat and cheese and veggies. I'd go to the bakery and get fresh buns. I'd come back and put everything together, and place the sandwiches in front of my mom and brother with pride.

The first day I did that, I felt accomplished. I could cook good food and wash the dishes, and I knew how to do my laundry. But it went even deeper than that. I didn't have a relationship with my dad. After the divorce, he was supposed to show up and pick us up one day a week, and he generally didn't. My mom was tired of that, and tired in general.

But despite everything that challenged her, Mom always put Donny and me first. She inspired me. So feeding my family allowed me to feel like I was satisfying something within me—I was giving back for all of the love and support Mom was giving me. I had a need that was truly fulfilled only by making those sandwiches. And even though I was only fumbling with bread and meat and veggies, I was also learning something really important about myself and the people around me. Giving something back to my mother and brother, even if that meant only saving her a small amount of time and money in making one meal, was something I embraced from the earliest moment I figured out how to put butter on bread.

Because of the meaning I got out of spending time helping my mom, I learned how to help others first.

I want you to understand how critical it is to front-end giving your time and effort to helping others.

This is more than that old adage of paying it forward. It's not a choice you should be making on a good day. It's crucial to give back to people in your community without expecting or getting anything in return every day. And you have to *constantly* and *consistently* give back, right from the start.

Many, if not most, businesses and leaders do it the other way around. Giving and helping usually comes *after* success, *after* the bills have been paid. Or it happens because there's a marketing incentive to support others, either personally or professionally.

Helping doesn't only mean giving time or money to charity. I love helping team members, entrepreneurs, friends, and family with a hand up for no other reason than that it feels good. It could be just being a friend to someone, or helping them understand where they fit in their community or company, or helping them find their unique space in the world.

Instead of thinking about creating success and then giving back, think about giving back to create success.

For me, giving back is about mentorship, perhaps precisely because that's the way I was supported.

So what exactly is mentorship?
It's not one thing. Mentorship can be a lot of things.

Most of us think about a mentor as someone who takes us under their wing because they know things we don't. That can still be the case. A classic mentoring relationship is one that looks a little like that, where a more experienced person gives advice and imparts wisdom to a less experienced person, either formally or informally.

Formal mentoring can look like a set schedule of meetings, or even a monthly check-in. Often, formal mentoring is set up within a business, where a senior team member is tasked with guiding a more junior person who has the potential to grow in their role, or it can consist of a board of advisors or a legal governing board. Formal mentoring can also take place within networking organizations, where people can seek out role models from among their more experienced peers.

Instead of creating success and then giving back, **give back to create success.**

Informal mentoring can happen anywhere and everywhere. Let's say you're at a conference and you see a great speaker in the hallway and pull them aside to ask an important question. Most professionals are willing to share their feedback and ideas if they have the time and mental space to do so.

Mass mentoring is on the rise because it can be tough to schedule one-on-one meetings or find the right mentor, and it can be a lot easier to share information in groups. This can include paid sessions in small groups with recognizable experts in their field, or it might look like a very specialized podcast or video series.

Finally, **peer mentoring** is when people at the same level of experience help each other out. This works especially in professions that are hands-on, like nursing, and a second set of eyes on a task can help prevent mistakes.

Mass Mentoring: Here You Go, Right Now

You want to access mass mentoring materials? I'm giving them to you for free, right now, and there is absolutely no catch. My mass mentoring partner—entrepreneur Greg Fleishman—and I know firsthand what it's like to start a consumer products business from scratch, moving to scale and ultimately to exit. And we want to support your entrepreneurial journey by sharing our own comprehensive database of resources through our Fata & Fleishman Mentorship community. Seriously, we're just giving it away. What you can find on fatafleishman.org:

• Capital-raising information with a list of more than 20,000 investors, and pitch deck templates

- Human resources documents for every function, including on-boarding, KPI scorecards, and templates for contracts, employee agreements, and corporate formation

- Business models, projection templates, legal documents, and equity models

- Marketing and brand strategy tools including trend studies, digital marketing tips, creative briefs, and research methods

- Sales planning models, distributor setup forms, and a boat-load of retailer lists, including supply chain demand forecast templates and a list of 3,300 co-packers

- Innovation and new product concepting frameworks

- A list of our recommended books with a comprehensive library of all key entrepreneur reading recommendations that worked for us

In any form of mentoring, whether you're the one with experience to share or the one looking for advice, it's not a straight shot to getting where you want to go.

See, a mentor can't actually solve a mentee's problems.

What a mentor can do is help a mentee grow into the person they want to be.

Think about the support you got early in life. Think about how you looked to your mother or your favorite uncle for advice. Your best teacher at school. If they were good at what they did in helping you become the person you are today, they didn't make your problems go away. They asked you the right questions. They pitched in when things got really hard, and helped you figure out your next step. They worked hard to make your day a little closer to best-day-ever status so that you felt good about your choices.

This is the goal of mentorship: *helping people decide what journey they want to take.*

In fact, there are a lot of people who have many mentors in their life. The best mentees are going to take insights from a range of people, teachings from different professors or gurus or however you categorize them, and then *internalize the ideas and choose what's best for them and for their business.*

That's the way to success.

Where it goes wrong is when people take literal direction from their mentors or coaches or any of the other people around them. That's because if there's even a couple of degrees of separation between their own goals and what their mentor's goals are in life, that could be a big enough gap for their advice not to work. Factors that lead to success change all the time and really depend on the resources we all have going for us.

So, if you want to mentor someone, you have to be focused on your mentee's needs. And what your mentee needs is confidence, understanding, and passion to see their ideas through.

If you want to be mentored, you have to be focused on your own personal growth, not on replicating someone else's.

I think about it as a giving circle.

Mentorship goes both ways. It gives back. Mentorship creates a relationship in which you're learning from and teaching each other.

More than that, mentorship creates the impetus for change in the world, making people, businesses, and communities open to new ideas through the free flow of information. We're going to delve into this idea more deeply later in the book, but I want to make sure you understand it right from the beginning: *embracing relationships with other people, and the mutual learning that comes with that, is the foundation for everything else you need to do to make your business work.*

It's kind of the opposite of what we think of when we found a business. We're used to hearing about competition, secret-keeping, patents, and lawsuits. We're taught that strategy means that we have to have a sustainable competitive advantage based on doing something that we protect at all costs from other folks in the business world.

But I'm here to tell you this: Creating a giving circle around your business, your ideas, and your team makes them stronger, not weaker. Giving to others, and giving back to your community, provides you with resources, support, and strength, both internally and with your future market.

The more giving you do, the larger your giving circle gets, which in turn provides everyone involved with countless new opportunities.

Where do you want your own giving circle to start?

There are three things you'll want to do, just to get going.

1   **Choose how you're going to mentor others.** What can you do right now that will change the way you interact with the people around you? What can you give? Is there something you love doing, even if you're not an expert, that you can share with others? Remember that mentorship is a two-way street, and you have to be prepared to give as much as you receive.

2   **Choose your own mentor.** How do you find a good mentor? Here are some suggestions based on my experience: Meet them on the field, as they are likely playing the same game. Attend trade shows and events, sign up for industry associations, angel networks, incubators, and accelerators. LinkedIn is also an awesome tool, but nothing beats meeting in person. Do you have a peer with whom you can

Mutual learning is the foundation for **everything you need to do to make your business work.**

partner to seek out resources to help you both thrive? Is there an equivalent to a joy-filled sandwich that you can offer up to those around you?

3   **Volunteer.** Make a difference outside of your personal success and business goals. Where can you use your skills? Where are they needed? What kind of organization or individual might benefit from your time? Or, even better, how can you find out who needs the most help? Start there.

Giving circles are important not only because they're going to get us somewhere in life. They also offer a high level of meaning in our work, and in our daily lives. Knowing that we can give our time and effort to help others allows us to build the kind of personal autonomy we need to make choices in a more fulfilling way. When we give to others, and they reward us with their trust, we begin to trust ourselves more: to connect, to experiment, and to trust in return. When we can build a sense of connection with others, it's a universal gift to ourselves. We're also learning, in turn, how to gain the support that each of us needs to succeed. A giving circle offers us the integration of work, of support, and of value creation.

And if you need proof, here's my reality. Giving circles are the foundation of who I am, and how I began to think about where I wanted to go next in life. In fact, right now, if I said the majority of my time is spent helping others, I wouldn't be exaggerating.

I built my success by giving back. Volunteering. Mentoring. Paying it forward. Treating people with the same kind of understanding and kindness I wanted to receive in return. Making that joy-filled sandwich. In doing it this way, I learned from the best.

And I'm still learning.

LESSON 3
HOW TO FEEL LIKE YOU

B Y THE TIME I was twelve, I hadn't felt like myself for a while.

Back in my first few years of school, I was doing really well. I had been placed with all the smart kids, three or four of them, in that special corner where we got to do extra reading and more challenging math. I remember that when I was four or five years old, one of the first things I said to my teacher was, "I already know all my pluses and minuses up to one hundred."

But in the classroom, just before I was supposed to go to high school, something changed. Slowly but surely, I transitioned from the smart corner to the bad corner. I was still getting bored in class and finishing my homework well before it was due, but I was having trouble not causing trouble.

I had also started smoking. Emotionally, smoking made me feel good, like I was successful or something. It started when one of the friends I hung out with got a pack of cigarettes, and we went down by the park away from the school to smoke, drink soda, and eat chips, thinking it was the coolest thing.

And I sure didn't have the healthiest diet. As a lower-income family, we had a tendency to over-rely on processed, high-calorie foods. For some reason, foods with added sugars, low dietary fiber, dyes, preservatives, and non-healthy fats are common in lower-priced meals. Especially back in the

'80s and '90s, the middle aisles of grocery stores were full of these options. Those sub sandwiches I'd been making seemed healthier, at least to me, because we were eating fresh compared to the Hamburger Helper and McDonald's that Mom relied on when we wanted a Friday night treat. But I didn't realize that the amount of food I was eating, the overindulgence of it, wasn't working well for my body. At the time, the physical satisfaction point for me wasn't one sub sandwich, it was four. I was a little chubby, but even so, Donny and I could work off most of the empty calories biking or walking to school and hanging out with friends.

But there was no going back after The Fight.

I was in no shape to fight the bully. A school-ground knock-out wasn't something I expected that day right after the bell rang. I knew it and he knew it. In fact, I had made the decision to walk away, to turn on my heel and just leave the scene. He didn't like that. The bully came up behind me and went to trip me, wrapping his leg around mine right behind my knee and pushing me over from behind. He came down hard with his weight behind me, pivoting to hold me down. Both bones in my leg twisted under his heavy body, enough that they snapped and kind of blew up—a compound fracture right up to the knee.

When I went down screaming, people started running out of the school.

"Get up!" the bully yelled at me, looking in fear at the principal striding toward him. "Get up!"

Bones pushed through my skin; there was blood everywhere. A teacher grabbed the bully by the elbow, and from the sirens, I knew someone had called an ambulance, but I don't remember much more than the searing pain.

At the hospital, they asked me the same questions paramedics had lobbed at me in the ambulance on the way there.

"What's your blood type?" they asked me, and my mother ran into the emergency room just in time to answer.

"Do you do drugs?"

"No," I said, gritting my teeth, feeling the tears I couldn't hold back streaming down my face.

"Smoke?"

I didn't answer.

"Do you smoke, kid?"

I looked up at Mom. "Yes," I admitted.

Mom's eyes widened. She hadn't known until that moment. Mom was a little bit naïve, but she was working overtime and counting on my brother to keep me in line.

I held out on having the break surgically fused with metal pins, even though it was what the doctors recommended. I was afraid of going under anesthesia. Mom felt my fear, and the doctors didn't press her too hard. But the damage was much more severe than they had anticipated.

They put a sixty-pound cast on, and when we got home, my leg was strapped to a board and I had to to stay in bed for three weeks straight, doctor's orders.

The painkillers I was on didn't help either. The fog of codeine made me tired, and it was also messing with my digestion. When I could hobble around, I didn't leave the house, especially when Mom was at work. I was told I had to stay in bed, I was told I had to heal, I was told I had to take these many pills every day if I was going to feel less pain.

But when the cast came off almost a year later, things weren't much better. My body wasn't getting what it needed to mend itself: movement, nutrition, hope. With the break as bad as it was, my leg just didn't work the same. There was atrophy, a limp. More painkillers. And I had barely been to school for the better part of my recovery period, so much so that I eventually decided not to go back at all.

I was riding a high of numbness.

Each day, I just became more lethargic. I didn't feel like doing anything but sitting or hanging out. Even as I eventually started moving again, I was still trapped in my addiction to both fast food and tobacco.

I was eating as an emotional response to phasing out of school and being alone at home. I found out that I could cook and made myself breakfast, filling my plate more and more every day—six or eight eggs, half a loaf of toasted bread, hash browns—enough for three or four people, and I ate it all. In fact, the more I cooked, the more I felt accomplished, like I had a skill I could practice.

It didn't take long for that aliveness to shift into a depressive cycle, though. With the processed foods I was eating, my body felt horrible and toxic and congested. I was bingeing and eating way too much, and then boomeranging into punishing myself and trying not to eat. It was a typical eating disorder, the kind that is rarely talked about among boys and men. Some days I would eat nothing; others, I would limit myself to one pint of ice cream instead of four. I even tried purging. Luckily, that never worked for me, because it would likely have triggered an even worse physical cycle. But the emotions were overwhelming and extreme. I swung from feeling like I was rewarding myself with pleasure and feeling I was in control to feeling lost and in physical pain from the amount of food I was putting in my teenage body.

I stopped weighing myself when I reached the top of the scale at three hundred pounds. I was only eighteen years old, and I felt like I was dying. My body physically hurt; the pain had been following me for half a decade already, but I had slowly become used to it. And by this point I was working in construction. It's a physical profession, and you'd think I might have needed the strength and stamina that comes with being

HOW TO FEEL LIKE YOU   **39**

in good shape. But in addition to the food and cigarettes I had never given up, there was partying and alcohol. Construction is also seasonal. There were months when all I did was watch movies, getting by on unemployment insurance.

Every day, I woke up feeling like shit, and I was sick all the time. There was a lot of physical pain. There was a lot of emotional trauma. There were binge-eating episodes every day. Life was a roller coaster ride and I just wasn't prepared to handle any kind of fluctuation. So I numbed myself, quieted my mind by checking out, not looking at my body, not allowing myself to recognize my pain.

There was a loneliness in being unhealthy that I couldn't shake.

It was another part of the equation that I hadn't admitted to myself up to that point—that deep sense of emotional pain that comes with disconnecting from your body. I really wanted a girlfriend who wasn't one of my friends, and one night at a party I looked over at my brother and his friends, happy and smiling, like they had the key to a secret. The world looked very different for them.

A friend of Donny's came up to me.

"Mike," he said as I was trying to light up another cigarette, like half the people in the room.

"Want one?" I offered.

"Mike, you're the laziest dude. Like, you need to change this shit out. This isn't going to be good," he said, giving me the once-over.

"What, smoking?"

"What, smoking?" he mocked me back. "I quit six months ago. You gotta stop."

I looked at him, and then I looked down at my hands, numb and tingling all the time, just like my feet. Besides being

I had to start with myself, and I had to know what I wanted **to see *in myself* before I could do anything else.**

lethargic and having no energy, I was lightheaded but still smoking a pack of cigarettes a day. We were all here, together, my friends, people I worked with. They were laughing, blissfully unaware of who I was in my own mind: exhausted, scared, worthless. I was in the same room as these happy, smiling people. We had the same interests, the same inside jokes. There wasn't anything substantially different about them compared to me, but I knew that they were happy. And I was not.

And then I hit my breaking point. I just didn't want to live like that anymore. I looked across the room at my brother again and made a decision.

I was sick and tired of being sick and tired.

In the mid-1990s, the biggest diet recommendation out there was to completely eliminate fat.

It was a fad diet, but it became bigger than that; non-fat was everywhere: in restaurants, on food labels, on covers of magazines. The grunge waif look was the status quo, and so to get rid of fat in our bodies, we all started taking fat out of our meals and snacks. What many people didn't yet realize was that companies were also switching out fat for sugar, changing out fat for more hidden calories. Health guru Nathan Pritikin was selling his vision of a non-fat future to newly thin superstars like Jennifer Aniston, and the media was full of success stories we all accepted as truth, no matter what was going on behind the scenes.

As I was starting to pay attention to all of this hype, I was feeling better. It took me eighteen tries to quit smoking, and I only switched up my daily McDonald's lunch for Subway, but it was a start. I asked my brother for help, and I started going to the gym every day. My brother and I started playing off each other, this healthy bodybuilding kind of lifestyle he had discovered. When I had first started gaining weight as a young teenager, he wasn't around so much. With that pretty typical age gap, his four years on me meant that he was out of the house and, well, not interested in even having a conversation with me. He was the cool guy, the popular guy. He had the beautiful girlfriend. I had one friend, a couch, and a frying pan. But all of a sudden, I had him back again—my brother, my mentor. Someone I could count on, someone who was there for me as I lifted weights for the first time, got on that treadmill.

Every day, I had a little bit more energy, a little more clarity, and I could feel it. I could feel myself becoming *me*.

I wasn't there yet, as you'll see. At the beginning, I wanted to see my brother in the mirror. But what I discovered was that I had to start with myself, and I had to know what I wanted to see *in myself* before I could do anything else.

So here is the basic thing you need to answer for yourself.

What do you want to see in *yourself*? What will make you truly feel like *you*? Because you can't have your best day unless you can actually conceptualize your best day.

And that best day may not be what you first imagine it to be. I mean, sitting on a beach is great. Meeting your friends for an after-work drink may feel good. But there's a cumulative effect that you're aiming for as well. When you're sitting on a beach to relax your mind and body once a week, that's helpful and comforting, but you're not going to feel good if that's what you're doing every single day. And while an after-work drink may feel good, yes, an after-work basketball game might feel better if it becomes part of your normal routine.

So what I'm talking about is figuring out the things that not only make you happy but also sustain you as a whole person: physical, mental, spiritual, or whatever makes you feel whole so that you can keep yourself feeling balanced and ready for what you're facing.

Here are the questions I've learned to ask myself so that I have my best day ever, every day.

1   **Who are my human resources?** I was the nerdy kid. I was the overweight kid. The poor kid. I didn't fit in. In my health journey, I didn't have an example to follow, an example of what eating well and taking good care of my body looked like. My mother was doing her best with the scant resources she had, just as all of us do. We were all working hard—Mom, my brother, and me—and when work was a chore, the flip side was to find something to satisfy ourselves quickly. Fast food, partying, watching movies. And worst of all, that forced relaxation at the end of the day after working for other people, making other people money, meant that we had all checked out, at least a little. We checked out before we even got to do what was important to us personally. Nothing changed for me until I allowed my brother to step back into my life and provide me with that deep support, something that cured my need to belong. The little confidence that I gained over the years of knowing he had my back meant that I trusted myself more and believed that I could find the answers I needed.

In your personal and professional life, find the right example to follow. You can find a new example of what inspires you, preferably a mentor you can trust and get to know, rather than someone on Instagram or Spotify. Who is that person? What does their day look like, every day? How do they make decisions? But more importantly, I don't want you to just do what they do. Instead, based on what looks attractive about their lives, I want you to discover some ideas that might be exciting to try and think about whether those ideas might be a fit for you and your daily life.

2 **Where are my knowledge resources?** For my personal journey, I was missing out on some of the key information we all need in order to have healthy diets. I latched on to fads because they were out there, showing me the way. But it wasn't until I educated myself, read some books, talked to people, and tried to find balance in my diet that I really started getting it. Typically, the human body is more like a juicer than it is a meat grinder. Fruits and vegetables cleanse and nourish our systems, and animal products strengthen them. We need only a bit of strengthening, but we need a lot of cleansing and nourishing.

   Educate yourself with evidence-based knowledge, not fads. If you want to discover your best day ever, what's the missing information you need? Sure, we often don't know what we don't know. That's why we get to examine what we know and test out different ideas. If you're interested in trying out a new exercise, actually try a few and see how they feel. You could hike instead of run, or try qigong instead of yoga. Go to the library and ask questions of an experienced librarian instead of looking online. Find resources that make sense for your choices, and take it slow.

3 **How can I find community resources?** I think there's a bigger picture here as well. It wasn't just my body that needed help. My mind was trapped as well. I was lonely, isolated, and, to be honest, not just numb, but scared of what might happen next. We need to support each other so that each of us can embody our own version of health on our own path. And I'm not talking about calling out each other's laziness like that bro-friend at my brother's party back in the '90s. I'm talking about finding that sense of belonging, surrounding yourself with people who care about you and want to see you find your center, your best self. That's

Only you are
in the best
position to look
at your situation
and **choose
the best
path for you.**

the hard part of all this, and the easiest as well: self-belief, patience, and self-care. Sometimes, belonging to a community just tips the scale enough to get on the path to your own best wellness journey.

No matter where you are on your path forward, the only thing you do need is a community. To truly live our best day ever, we need to feel like we *belong* to something. Everyone's life journey is different, but—and here's the big lesson—everyone should feel like they fit in. We need examples of what a good life looks like in our lives, but more than that we need to circle each other with support. What kind of community do you want to join or form? Where do they hang out? What would hanging out with this community look like for you?

4   **How can I be me, no matter what?** I know that many people try to emulate my own health journey, but I can't tell you what to do. I can tell you what I would do if I was in your situation. Just like the fallacy of fad diets, there's not just one way to do it. Fad diets get passed around because they're an easy way for us to understand what to do next, but it also means that we belong to a club of believers. Everyone's in the same boat, and it feels good to belong to a group. But here's the thing. Everybody, every *body*, is different. While truly balanced diets, like the Mediterranean way of eating I follow now, work for most people, that's not always the case. And not everyone has the ability to follow a strict physical regimen of any kind because of their own personal limits, their mental or physical limitations that they can't change. And that's okay.

Only you are in the best position to look at your situation and choose the best path for you. Popular lifestyle plans need to be set aside for more personalized solutions based on our own needs, our own goals, and what works for us. In fact, the beauty of learning to care for your own needs is that you don't have to do what I do. Knowing what you know about yourself, ask yourself what would feel good right now. What would make your mind, your body, your emotional self feel good?

Now that you have some human, knowledge, and community resources, and you're starting to think about what might make your life that little bit better, try it out. Change up your day. *Start* with the good things. Don't wait until you're tired after work if you don't want to. Front-end the best things in life. See if giving yourself a few life choices first thing in the morning affects your mood, your energy levels.

You *get to* learn about your own life's desires. Your own body. You're allowed to discover what you want, and how to walk that path. You can *choose* your own community, your own mentors, and learn what works for you.

In order to do what I do, I found my passion for health. When you take care of your body and it's not processing fear and the challenges that come with that stress, things begin to shift. You can feel safe in reaching out to others, because then they get to reach back, and it creates a circle of trust. You can discover what you love to eat because of how it feels, and how you love to move because *it moves you*.

Enjoy this journey. It's yours alone.

LESSON 4
KNOW YOUR PASSION

LOSING WEIGHT over the next two years, I totally bought into the dream.

At the same time, I took on another kind of eating disorder—one of control, one of extremes, and one that led to anorexia.

It was an accident. I eventually completely eliminated fat from what I ate. I was so convinced that I was doing the right thing for myself, for my body. But I was becoming so thin that people started to notice. The same guys who called me out for being lazy were taking stock of my leanness. At six feet tall, I had dropped from three hundred pounds to 160. My hair started falling out, my complexion was horrible, and my body was covered in eczema. I couldn't digest food. I was starving myself of fat, and it started to really show. I thought I was doing everything right until I realized how very wrong I was. How dependent I was on an extreme way of thinking, how I was lacking any sense of balance. How tied I had become to a fear of getting fat again.

I remember getting to a point where I had accidentally cut my hand and it wouldn't stop bleeding until a couple of hours had passed. It wasn't good.

I wasn't healthy.

Again.

A few days after I cut my hand, I found myself walking through the door of my local health food store, searching for answers.

The kind-hearted woman behind the counter handed me a copy of Udo Erasmus's 1993 book, *Fats That Heal, Fats That Kill*. She turned to a chart in the book. It outlined what happens to your body if you don't get enough omega-3s—essential fatty acids—in your diet.

Your hair falls out. *Check.* Your skin looks terrible. *Check.* Your digestion tanks. *Check.* Your blood doesn't clot. Uh, yeah, that cut on my hand still was bleeding through the bandages five days after the knife slipped.

Hmmm.

I felt duped. The whole low-fat diet thing wasn't real. It was a scam. Nathan Pritikin didn't have the full story, even though he was selling books as an expert, a doctor, someone who was supposed to know everything about his subject matter. I followed his rules, the rules everyone was following, and I ended up with a serious essential-fatty-acid deficiency.

But here, in my hands, was the instruction manual for my next level of health, or at least part of the story that I had never heard about before. The curtain got pulled back. I had to do my own research and test out new ideas. I had to keep my mind open and look for what worked for me, for my body.

Udo Erasmus had other lists and charts, including the ten best foods that I needed to get those fatty acids into my system. Food number two, and everything lower on the list, was available in that health food store. Number two was flaxseed oil, which I bought immediately. It was shining off the shelf in my direction, like the beacon of healing I needed right at that moment. I shared my findings with my brother, my gym friends, anyone who would listen.

But that elusive number one source of what I needed to become healthy wasn't in that health food store because it wasn't being produced, at least not to the mass market.

In Erasmus's book, flax was number two, and hemp was number one.

As a teenager growing up in the early '90s, I always thought hemp was cool.

In that way, I was a pretty normal kid. But when I bought into the cannabis vibe, I went all in: Bob Marley, reggae, medicinal uses of cannabis, recreational cannabis, the hemp movement. I felt a kind of alliance with this plant. It had been kept down, forced out of the status quo for fifty years, and it was even called "weed." And yet it also was a special plant. It made people feel good. I didn't ever feel like I fit in, and so I related to it: cannabis was unconventional, just like me.

After learning the cold, hard fact that hemp was number one in terms of its nutritional value, its *value to our bodies*, the cannabis plant took on a whole other level of meaning for me—a deeply spiritual meaning. Sure, I had fixed my essential-fatty-acid deficiency with flaxseed oil, but what if I could do better? What if I could actually follow the best-source plan?

Suddenly, I recognized that hemp was Mother Nature's gift: it could heal not only my own body but *everyone's* bodies. All the political stuff surrounding hemp was a kind of nonsense from the past. I could be its champion.

It was that exact moment that I truly fell in love with hemp.

And just in case you need to know, cannabis plants include both psychoactive varieties and non-psychoactive varieties. Here's what I mean by that. Cannabis rich in tetrahydrocannabinol, or THC, is known as marijuana because THC is the molecule that makes people high. Cannabis with low THC is

I recognized that hemp was Mother Nature's gift: **it could heal not only my own body but *everyone's* bodies.**

called hemp. Hemp contains cannabidiol, also known as CBD, as well as essential fatty acids and a host of other nutritional benefits that are still being discovered through research. Both CBD and THC are health-promoting molecules, but health food and medical products that are made from hemp are not psychoactive, meaning that the level of THC in the plant is very low.

Hemp is often misunderstood. Once you get down those basic facts, though, it's a lot less controversial than it seemed back in the '90s.

At the time I began healing my body, I started sharing my progress with my friends from the gym. I had started reading bodybuilding magazines, and their focus was always on improvement. Recommendations like having a protein shake with egg whites were pretty much par for the course. Flax fit into that kind of mindset, and everyone around me was super-excited about how my body was changing for the better. I didn't just put back on some of the weight I had lost in my extreme bid for self-confidence, but I also performed better in the gym. That meant my friends were paying close attention to my new eating plan because they wanted to see the same results for themselves.

But in the back of my mind, I thought I could do even better. The first-place position hemp was in meant it had to be better for my body than second-place flax.

There was another idea driving my thoughts as well. As I was getting my health plan balanced out and back on track, I had also stopped drinking alcohol. Cannabis was the only external buzz I allowed myself to enjoy. At the same time, society's view of cannabis had started to shift a little, and it was becoming less countercultural and more an expected part of our lives. In the beginning, I tried cannabis because of the high. But as I grew up and as that perception shift took place, at the end of the night I would start thinking about how cannabis allowed me to be open to new insights into how we live, and about how I made choices that allowed me to thrive.

And it wasn't just self-reflection. Understanding the plant itself meant that I wanted to be out in the woods. I got into gardening. I became truly interested and invested in Mother Nature and feeling really connected to the world around me. I wanted to cultivate and protect plants and everything they were able to offer humankind.

In that state of mind, I decided that I needed to reach out and do something. I needed to follow my passion. I needed to change the way we all thought about hemp. Because I believed in hemp, I needed to share hemp with the world.

Unconventional paths do lead to success.

I had been hanging around a hemp store in Winnipeg, one of those hippie, pop-culture-type deals, since I was a teenager. It was a no-brainer to reach out to the two owners of the store, Martin and Alex, to get the real scoop on whether or not it was possible to locate food-grade hemp.

Closing in on a decade older than me, Martin and Alex were the real deal. They were Winnipeg's cannabis counterculture experts and had been working solidly to reach out to the broader public for a couple of years, aiming to make sure that hemp became legal sometime soon. In fact, at the time I approached them, they were involved in a publicly traded company, Consolidated Growers & Processors (CGP), and they had just started to create new hemp products that met the criteria of the legislation they helped change.

I came on as an investor. That sounds loftier than it was at the time. I was working the night shift at the *Winnipeg Free Press* newspaper production offices loading papers and had a few thousand dollars to sink into this idea. My brother and a bunch of our friends also decided to come on board. I spent every penny I had on CGP.

It was more sweat than equity. It wasn't just an investment. In fact, my plan was to create my own brand of hemp foods and buy raw hemp product from CGP, kind of like a strategic alliance. I essentially ran the brand out of my mom's house, in my bedroom, on my mom's computer. I really didn't know what I was doing. But it felt good, no matter where I was, no matter how difficult it was. Playing and building something with hemp felt like a free pass to something amazing I couldn't quite name.

Martin and Alex had some contacts, especially their provincial funding partners, who made it possible to test out ideas. I connected with the Food Development Centre in Portage la Prairie in Manitoba (which unfortunately just lost its provincial funding at the time I started writing this book). There, I met Alphonsus Utioh, a research leader who I would say is the godfather of Manitoba Harvest, and one of the greatest examples of what mentorship looks like. Through his guidance, I learned everything about how to put a product together, how to do that first production run, how to use bottling and labeling equipment, where to buy the jars and other supplies, how to get grants to cover our expenses in the lean first few years. Everything. Sure, I was already a health food consumer, but I was also a complete newcomer to the business world, and Alphonsus made everything work. Including me.

I figured out pretty quickly that my own shopping habits could serve the business. The first shop that bought our hemp oil, which is what we started out selling, was the same health food store where I'd bought Erasmus's book: the Canadian Nutrition Centre. The store was literally across the street from Mom's place.

"Can you do me a favor and put a few bottles on the shelf?" I asked.

Marvin, the store owner, shook his head. "I'm not getting a request for hemp oil. No one's asking for it."

But I was a good customer. I was in every week.

"Marvin, you gotta give it a try."

"Nope."

The sixth time I went in after the first ask, I told him I wasn't going to give up.

"All right, Mike," Marvin said, looking at me like I was crazy. "Give me three bottles."

I went back to my mom's place and returned with the bottles and a little invoice booklet. I invoiced him for $22.50, which he then paid me out of the cash register.

The next day, I sent a few of my friends from the gym to Canadian Nutrition Centre. They bought all of the product off the shelf.

The day after that, I was back with another three bottles. That time, Marvin didn't hesitate to unlock the till.

The quickest leap forward is the one you imagine for yourself. It wasn't more than three or four months later when we merged my business, Red River Valley Hemp Company, fully with Emperor's Clothing Company, and, in creating Fresh Hemp Foods, rebranded ourselves as Manitoba Harvest Hemp Foods.

"So, Mom," I remember saying to start the conversation. "I'm gonna get into the hemp business and start this company. Well, I'm kind of going to invest in this other company and *then* start this company."

To her credit, Mom didn't blink. We secured an office downtown. That's when it became real.

When we got the keys to the place, the first thing she asked was, "What do you need from me?"

"Seriously?"

If you are really passionate about a project, **you won't accept anything less than amazing.**

"You're probably going to need to secure some operating credit," she said matter-of-factly. "I'll co-sign. A computer and some office furniture, for sure."

"Um, yes. Yes!"

Mom even invested in the first production run. It's not as if I grew up in a family where production was in our genes. We didn't have factories and farms. As you know, I grew up with no money. We just had each other—and a deep commitment to changing the future we imagined for ourselves.

I created an experimental run first. I made one hundred bottles of hemp oil with hand-written labels, all packaged up on my mom's apartment dining room table, which is probably why Marvin at the Canadian Nutrition Centre looked at them kind of funny. Later, at the Food Development Centre, we packaged up a run of 1,000 bottles. We got some labels professionally printed that time. But we still didn't have a big enough fridge to keep a thousand bottles in, so we ended up storing them at my brother's house in a spare basement bedroom with the window cracked open.

In the office, as well, I still felt like an outsider. My first conversation with the administrative person from Consolidated Growers & Processors who was helping us out . . . well, it was very awkward.

"Hey, I need to write this company a letter. I'm not sure how it's supposed to go," I said to her. At that moment, the fact that I hadn't been in school since I was thirteen suddenly felt overwhelming.

"You're like, 'Dear so and so,'" she offered kindly. "And then you write some paragraphs of information, ask them what you need."

"I didn't know," I said, looking down.

"Of course, Mike. That's how it goes. It's okay. I'll read it afterward, before you send it out."

I recall having money for the day when I was a kid: enough for a hamburger and a pack of cigarettes and a Coke. When I started working in the '90s, I realized that I had money for the week, or the month, or even for three months. But when I calculated the sales for the business, I realized that I could sell $1,500 of product per day by contacting new stores, new friends of friends, and making the pitch for healthy living through hemp. If I were dialing for dollars, I could afford to take the leap to having a year's worth of resources saved instead of just three months' worth.

But I was doing nine-to-five at the Manitoba Harvest office and then working from 10:30 p.m. to 3:30 a.m. at the *Free Press*. I was getting only a handful of hours of sleep a night, power napping at midday, and then balancing that with trying to be super-healthy. But I realized more each day that it was possible for the business to be the full hustle. I could let my previously full-time gig slide. The salaried work I was doing was a distraction. Instead of sixty hours a week working the business and up to forty hours at the newspaper factory (swinging some overtime when I needed it), if I put all one hundred hours into the business, I might be able to make it work.

I started thinking about what that could look like for me. I'd be able to move out of my mom's house, rent an apartment downtown a block away from our business, and then just go full in.

But first, I needed a cash cushion large enough to prove it could be done.

If money motivates you, sorry to tell you: you likely won't make it.

Here's where we're going to slow down for a second.

Too many entrepreneurs are looking for immediate success.

I'll say that again, in a different way: Money does not matter in the way a lot of people think it does. If you're an entrepreneur or a CEO, accumulating money should not be on your agenda. Because if you focus on getting rich, rather than focusing on what you can *do* with money to follow your passion in life, you will fail.

I want to make this clear as well: You have to be focused on the right thing. What is your *personal* passion? Not the corporation's passion, not the shareholders' passion: *your* passion. If you're working on a project you're passionate about, you can just do it forever. And you won't be doing it forever because you're lounging about in blissful happiness and accepting whatever outcome you end up with. It's the opposite of that.

If you are passionate about a project, you want to do it well every day. You want the kind of excellence that big companies *wish* they had. The *idea* of excellence that gets printed on inspirational posters in corporate hallways but is often never reached because people just don't care enough to aim for it.

If you are really passionate about a project, there's no way you can fail. Because you will keep trying until you get everything right, working till you succeed at whatever metric is important to *you.*

If you are really passionate about a project, you won't accept anything less than amazing. Your project will be amazing because you have a reason to get up in the morning, to create, to innovate, and to thrive.

Every day, I live my passion as an entrepreneur. I'm lucky, though, because I work in the natural products industry, and we see a lot of passion for what we do. People become passionate about their work because of a change to their health brought on by creating and using products that positively affect people's health. These entrepreneurs want to talk about their products all day, all night, so why not offer their positive lived experience to the world?

That's exactly my experience as well. I went from literally walking around telling people, "Don't eat fat. Fat is bad for you," to "Oh, I made a mistake, we all need essential fatty acids. Here, try this." It was critically important for me to share my story and my reason for surviving my childhood trauma and its effect on my physical self and mental health.

When you do follow your passion, you need to expect that there will be failure, growth, and a lot of change along the way. Because that will make you even better at your passion. We have this feeling that failure is final. As soon as we fail, it's done. We're finished. There's no more.

In fact, making mistakes only really occurs when we stop or give up. Otherwise, we're talking about learning.

The route toward our passions goes through testing and discovering, making mistakes and getting back up again. We have to become powerful at setting aside our expectations so that we're authentically diving into who we are; so that we're creating space to answer questions we're passionate about. We have to become powerful at letting ourselves explore our passions and look for places to learn.

There is no reason for you to settle for working on a business that does not inspire you, even if you started that business yourself. Creating a business just to make money, or even to meet some random market need that doesn't really matter to you personally, will not position you for success. Instead, identify what makes you content and what inspires you, and be conscious about and present in what's happening around you, so that you can develop the bravery to really dive in.

Start out by looking for an example of what a good business, a passion-inspiring business, might look like for you. Remember, you're aiming to create your best day ever, every day. Start there, and then think about next steps that allow you to learn more about what matters to you, and what you want to do every single day. Ask yourself things like:

- What is one thing I'd want to do every day, forever?

- How can I learn more about how to follow my passion?

- How can I find resources or support in a way that allows me to embody my passion?

- Who are five people I know who are passionate about the same thing?

- What does that passion mean to other people, and what do they need?

- Perhaps most importantly, who are the passionate people already working in this field, and how can I seek them out for their advice?

And if you don't start following your passion?

When you're working hard at your "non-passion" and your inbox is overflowing, you are not making any progress. You're not getting anywhere. You've got this thing that you want to do, this calling, this idea that's bigger than you, and when you look at your to-do list and none of those things is going to get you any closer to that calling, it doesn't feel good or right. What that means is that the very best of you is *not* being called upon to solve a problem *you actually care about*. You're not being psychically or financially rewarded for the things that matter to *you*.

The money you need to survive and thrive will come in if you want to show up to the business you create every day. But even more importantly, the money will come in if you show up *for yourself*.

You are what you need to be passionate about.

LESSON 5
MAKE FRIENDS FIRST

THERE'S A moment in every newsroom pundit speech, every business school curriculum, and even during some pub table debates, when Sun Tzu's *The Art of War* is offered up as a pathway to business success.

More than 2,500 years ago, Chinese master strategist Sun Tzu wrote this book about navigating through battle successfully, the first tenet of which was that you must know the enemy and yourself. Although originally meant to offer wisdom for generals, dozens of *Forbes* and *Wired* magazine articles argue that the book is as relevant to today's global business landscape as it was to ancient battlefields because it reads like a how-to for a multinational consumer products company. B-school professors argue that market competition is like a war, a never-ending one, and that we can use this text as a means of gathering, analyzing, synthesizing, and using information to make better decisions and take more effective action on the field of play because business is like a military hierarchy.

It makes sense to some because most of what we've created in the modern business world is a result of what we learned in World War II: innovating on the fly, creating warehouses of extra goods, developing global distribution partnerships, and anticipating people's needs before they're even stated out loud. Our terms of play on the battlefield got moved right into the boardroom.

Yeah ... no.

A war only exists if we're fighting—and we don't need to fight to win. What we need in business isn't war. It's authentic human connection. It's trust. It's friendship.

In 1998, a random company didn't show up at the Winnipeg Wellness Expo.

We'd been running Manitoba Harvest for a few months when I got a call. There was a booth available at the province's largest health consumer show. Except that it wasn't really a booth. It was kind of a table, or more like half a table. A much larger company had intended this small extension for one of their strategic partners, who canceled at the last minute. A friend was there and thought we might be the kind of people who'd show up to a random sales opportunity, and he was right.

With hemp oil as our only product and a lot of misinformation out there, we wanted to make sure people understood that we weren't selling drugs under that two-foot table end. We had just bought a printer, which we thought was pretty fancy. Given that the Internet was just starting to roll out, we basically downloaded some doodles and created what we thought was a pretty cool illustration of what Manitoba Harvest was all about. We designed this little black-and-white brochure on our office computer, all about the three types of fats—saturated, monounsaturated, and polyunsaturated—and why we all need essential fatty acids. "That's all we need," we thought to ourselves. We were good to go.

It was a three-day show. As it was my first consumer show, I had no idea what it would be like to spend eight hours each day just talking to people. But what I realized quickly was that my own personal story was the best talking point I had.

I rolled out the whole story quickly to anyone who'd listen: "I used to weigh three hundred pounds and I lost one hundred pounds, but I learned a whole bunch about fat, and you need fat. So if you're afraid of fat, you should take this brochure."

Over that weekend, I sold three hundred bottles of the 1,000-bottle run. The retail price was $10, so we made $3,000 in sales—our biggest amount yet.

But that wasn't the best thing that happened.

First, I got super pumped up talking to people about Manitoba Harvest, because it meant talking about health: theirs and mine. I realized that health was my favorite thing to talk about because people want to figure out their own health path, and I have some experience figuring out my own. I felt needed, I felt helpful, and it made me excited to think that I was on my own right path.

Second, I found out that I was with my people. The floor was filled with founders or smaller business owners or the people who were working with them. As a health food consumer, I thought that was the coolest thing because I could talk to people who wanted to reach the same goals and had the same interests as me. It was like joining a special club made just for me.

Third, I discovered that making friends could equal making big business and big life changes. John Holtmann, owner of seven stores under the Vita Health brand in Manitoba, the largest and most successful health food store chain of its kind at the time, came over to our booth.

"Hey," he said, "all my customers keep coming over from your booth to see me. They bought hemp oil."

"Do you want one of our brochures?" I asked, handing him one. I started telling him my story.

He nodded. "We need to have this in the store," he said, handing me his card. "Come see me first thing next week."

There are different forms of learning, **different ways to educate yourself.**

Manitoba Harvest went from being stocked at only Marvin's store to suddenly adding seven more locations. Even more than that, John became a mentor of mine and one of our first shareholders.

That day changed my life. When I look back at it now, I know that show was instrumental in launching the company.

More than that, it was the start of a community.

Mentoring is a committed friendship connected to a community.

Given my history with the education system, I was a little bit against school. So when the door was opened to a mentoring relationship with John, it really changed the way I thought about learning: there are different forms of learning, different ways to educate yourself. In fact, you can seek out your own teachers and professors in life. You can learn from people with your specific interests in mind, and cater to your own skill set.

But that wasn't clear to me in the beginning, at least with my education-focused terminology. What I did know was that I was a sponge, and I still am.

My most-used personal calls to action sound something like this:

- I *need to learn* how to do this.
- When I do this, what does *good look like*?
- What's the *highest-quality* way to do this?
- What does the *world-class* way to do this look like?
- What are the skills I need to easily *blueprint* this?

The thing is, however, it's impossible to address almost any of these calls to action without making friends first. You can't force a mentor to show up for you. You have to build that relationship. My great advantage is that I don't hesitate to reach out to new people, meet up with them, and ask them questions.

Let's take the example of when I had to set up our first website. And keep in mind, we're still talking about the '90s. I knew I *needed to learn* how to do something on the Internet, which was what *good looked like*. So I learned through a friend how to write HTML code. Back then, knowing HTML was the *highest-quality* approach to putting up a website. But then we took it one step further and went *world class*. We actually built a web store in 1999, which was really early-adopter level when it came to online sales. The literal minute that I made the store live, we got our first order. I knew only then that I had the skills to keep going and *blueprint* our next wave of growth.

Achieving this win felt like one of those many things in my life that had meaning: we were on the right path.

Here's where my consumer and trade show friendships fit into the big picture.

Starting up, there were a lot of regulatory uncertainties with hemp, even though it was legal in Canada. The idea was so fresh that no one knew what the rules really were or weren't. We had to be licensed to manufacture and sell hemp; our farmers had to be licensed to grow hemp. So we actually formed a hemp *industry association*, including lots of our own competitors in the mix. We had to make it work, and we needed each other.

We also needed some stability for the people farming our hemp. So when we brought John on as a mentor and learned from what he did in the health food industry, we knew we needed more folks on our team. We reached out to twenty farmers to invest in the company as well, which gave us a pretty strong agricultural base going forward. Our *network of growing partners* expanded outside of Manitoba to Alberta and Saskatchewan.

And let's not forget our *friendships in the hemp community*. The people interested in hemp were our first bull's-eye target.

Like me, they were going to hemp stores to buy all their hemp stuff. Before hemp became more mainstream and was available in all the stores, I knew we had to be authentic, talk to those customers, and understand why they were early adopters.

You may think, "Hey Mike, these aren't your friends, they're your business contacts." But that's honestly not how I see it. There's an authenticity that arises when you connect with someone who actually cares about the same things you do. That connection goes beyond business. It's about a shared value system that reaches deep, and it means that even when I meet someone for the first time, we have the potential to be actual friends, not just business acquaintances looking for a way to make money together. What we're actually looking for is a way to help each other, help others, and build our lives' daily practices around health. It's a rich way of living, whether or not it creates financial wealth.

For me and my cofounders, this mantle of people, our friends, became our family. And these friendships allowed me to find mentors in every relationship I created.

More friendship equals more mentorship.

People always ask me, "Where can I find a mentor?" And I say that everyone has to look for a mentor on the field because they're likely playing the same game you are. Go to the trade show, go to the industry association, to the non-profit organization, to any activity that interests you. Go to where those people hang out because that's where you're going to find them.

My initial consumer show experience was so powerful that I knew we needed to do more shows. It was kind of ridiculous: the next show we did was the Christmas Craft Show, just because I felt like I had to get back out there right away. But then I dove right in: I went to health shows all across Canada, including the Victoria Health Show, the Vancouver Health Show, the Calgary Health Expo, the Winnipeg Wellness Show, and the Total Health Show in Toronto.

Now, my consumer and trade show secret is to show up early in the morning. If you have an exhibitor badge, you can get in before the show opens for setup, and then you can see everyone's booth for a couple of hours before everything gets crazy-busy. Even now, I love to check out what's happening with different brands, to see what's new and amazing. Lately, it's been all about plant-based meats, all new brands. In the past, it was coconut oil and cold-brewed coffee.

But every year there's some true innovation, and a chance for me to start mentoring someone else.

Not long ago, I noticed a new booth at Natural Products Expo. It was the smallest size at the show, ten feet by ten feet, and the company was called Mid-Day Squares. The crowd around their booth was constantly buzzing. While the product was a big hit, offering up functional-food chocolate snacks, it was their energy that drew me in. With a whole video crew, they were filming people trying out their snacks, radiating positive vibes and inclusion, and engaging everyone around them as they uploaded live to social media. And they just killed it. They landed a distribution deal with major national customers in the United States and won an award at the show at the same time. But what was behind that energy was even more impressive. They had a story to tell—about health and the need for joy in life, for taking a midday break to stop and look after ourselves. Their approach was storytelling first and delivering the product second, instead of focusing on the product experience alone.

Of course, I wanted to meet the folks behind Mid-Day Squares and hear about what they wanted to do with their product. Lezlie Karls; her husband, Nick Saltarelli; and her

Business comes second. **Always. Be a person of the people.**

brother Jake Karls launched Mid-Day Squares in 2018. A few years earlier, Lezlie had been watching Nick knock back his daily Oh Henry! candy bars and thought that she might be able to come up with a better, plant-based alternative. And wow, she really did.

"We're a functional-chocolate company," Nick told me. "But the next question always is, 'What is functional chocolate?' It's relooking at what a legacy company like Hershey's or Cadbury might be doing if they started building their business today, from scratch. What we want is a product that makes us feel really good when we're done eating it. And so it's not intended to be anything more than a chocolate bar. We're not trying to be an energy bar. We're a modern chocolate company. That's the elegance."

Nick is right. It is an elegant idea to rethink legacy brands and systems. There's no reason for us to keep going back to prop up old companies that don't serve a modern point of view. It's not about dropping trendy ingredients into old brands; it's about designing something that suits our lives right now.

Better products can also mean better processes. What I like about Mid-Day Squares is that they are big believers in owning their entire production process from start to finish, which gives them the ability to scale up. But the team is also emotionally invested in their own product, which means that they're building emotional connections with the people who buy their products as well.

"The more the people who buy our products connect with us, the more they see that our brand is not just a brand. We're human," Nick said. "Traditional marketing, those tools brands used to use to manipulate an audience ... I don't know anymore. I think companies are starting to figure that out."

And as the Mid-Day Squares team suggests, consumers are figuring that out as well. Buying legacy-brand chocolate means that consumers have to buy into a production system where farmers, crop loads, and the environment are suffering; where consumers themselves are suffering from the overload of sugar and cheap ingredients in legacy brands' constantly rejigged recipes to cut costs.

What modern consumers really want in food is a product they love: something that tastes amazing that doesn't ask them to give up flavor, and that makes them feel good in terms of their health and ideal future. Sure, you could try and find a middle ground, but why? Especially if, like Mid-Day Squares, you can make it your mission to ensure that your chocolate not only meets those consumer values but also is at a price point that works. There will be a tipping point where all businesses will start thinking this way. We shouldn't just want to create brand value. We need to create human value, because our buyers, our communities, won't stand for anything less.

Not settling for less? That's what friendship is really about, too.

One of my ultimate strengths is my friendships. Friendship just feeds off itself. People say that I'm very easy to hang out with, but that's because I've made the best day for myself. It's me showing up instead of the worst version of myself. Part of what makes me stay focused on having my best day ever, every day, is that it allows me to connect with people in a relaxed, kind, and compassionate way.

That's why you have to open yourself up to doing things that make sense to you as a whole person, and to reaching out to others who want to take the journey with you.

Compartmentalizing your business as a job is different from seeing entrepreneurship as a lifestyle, too. It's not the old, "Hey, can I have fifteen minutes of your time because I'd like to sell you something?" Not at all. It's about starting to understand each person we meet with one conversation at a time and letting it develop naturally. If you have friendships, true relationships, in your work, doing business is just that much easier. Not only is it a way to get things done, but also you end up out-competing others who rely on the old sales schtick and who just aren't going to put themselves out there as genuine people.

In our work, we can build solid relationships, real friendships, for the long term. If you think about it from a business standpoint, there are relationship opportunities all the way through your whole business, internally and externally, and the same is true for all parts of our lives. Every day I take the time to connect, communicate, and listen—despite the fact that I started out as an introvert—because I want to share my story. And so does everyone else. People really want to connect authentically and deeply, and that's the starting point to building a movement, and a legacy.

A military mindset in business comes from a place of scarcity and fear. But there doesn't have to be a series of battles either inside or outside companies if our friendships are built to help us truly thrive in our communities, and if people are where they're supposed to be. Starting with friendship means that we're all acting from a place of confidence and discovery. Life isn't about being the best at something and beating our competitors, it's about learning how to adapt to all of the changes we will constantly face in every aspect of our working life, but also every moment we are alive.

Friendship makes us the best at something. What a beautiful lack of fear, of effort, of conflict, when nothing is in the way of our human nature, our actualization, and our trust of each other.

Business comes second. Always.

Be a person of the people.

LESSON 6
BELIEVE IN YOUR OWN VISION

YOU THINK successful people don't feel imposter syndrome? Think again.

Even with a lot of new sales coming in the door at the turn of the new millennium, we were still learning. The learning curve was especially steep when we had to ramp up production. We were increasing product batches, and, for whatever reason, the product was just okay.

Okay wasn't good enough. Not at all.

We had to make the hard decision to stop selling that product, even to the point of taking a loss, one that had a significant financial impact on the business at the time. As a young entrepreneur, especially as someone who had emerged from childhood poverty, I was understandably nervous. It felt like a threat. I felt like I was going to drown.

But I had to uphold what the Manitoba Harvest brand was going to stand for long term, and while other elements for my vision would emerge over time, the first thing I knew was that the brand was going to stand for quality.

My vision for quality was honed by that same need to ensure that my products were healthy and contributing something positive to people, to the world. But I was also inspired by what I had read and learned about the Toyota method.

Coming back to one of my essential questions, namely, what did the *world-class* way to do business look like, I found out that a world-class quality culture looked like a Toyota production line. I had read about Toyota in some magazine I picked up on a flight back in the '90s, and the lesson stuck. In Toyota's just-in-time speak, Kanban was an effective tool in support of running a production system as a whole, because every employee could mark a problem using a yellow sticky note wherever they saw a flaw. Even to this day, anyone on that production line can pull the handle and the whole production line stops. Quality assurance at Toyota means that every problem is addressed right here and now.

Seeing what was happening on our production line, I decided to bring that vision of quality to Manitoba Harvest. I wanted to make sure anyone could stop the line if there was something wrong.

But before you can stop the line, you have to get a few things right.

At Toyota, their vision of quality is literally printed on the walls. It's printed on T-shirts, on people's job descriptions, on their training documents. It's so much a part of their culture that Toyota's organizational framework is deliberately flattened. Everyone is seen as an integral part of the team. That team integrity, literally, is part of the goodwill, the brand, and the value of that business today.

So that's what we homed in on at Manitoba Harvest, building a culture that had quality as one of its core values. Despite the added worry of the cost, we highly invested in process and quality management systems and training. We eliminated gatekeepers to change management. We became really clear with what was going to be acceptable to our customers, and what was going to be acceptable to our company values. We deputized everyone to be a quality sheriff throughout the business.

Hemp health was a lifestyle that not everyone was aware of at the time, and especially the idea of promoting health all day long. That was brand-new. That was Manitoba Harvest's ethos. But barely anyone outside of the alternative-health community was following a vegetarian or plant-based diet when we were ramping up. Focusing on quality, however, we soon learned that the majority of the team felt proud that they were working in a business that was making the world a healthier place by offering hemp products to all. We were also beginning to see all of the positive feedback from consumers and testimonials about our socially and environmentally responsible business.

That's when the quality mark we were aiming for began to feel real.

In fact, we soon discovered that the number one reason people wanted to work at Manitoba Harvest was the same as my own reason: personal and professional growth. The number two reason was that they could be proud of the work they were doing—so much so that they'd tell their family and friends about that pride.

With a shared vision, none of us hesitated in living the brand because it was meaningful for all of us.

It's a little strange, setting up a vision for other people and their futures.

It feels a bit outrageous and problematic in some ways to ask anyone else to follow your lead. It's a bit demanding, especially when you're paying someone else's salary, to tell them what ought to be important in their day-to-day life.

But here's the thing. Setting up a vision for a company doesn't have to look like a demand, or even an ask. It doesn't require you to even be visionary or to act like you know what you're talking about. Setting up a vision can be a natural evolution of the community and friendships you've already established inside and outside of the company.

Setting up a vision can be a natural evolution of the community and **friendships you've already established.**

At Manitoba Harvest, we were awarded the highest level of food safety and quality certification in the world: BRC (British Retail Consortium) Global Standards AA+. We even won awards for our utilization of the program. We were overwhelmed by comments from BRC management auditors in our facility who were shocked that our quality assurance wasn't run by a specialized quality office; it was quality assurance run by the whole team. Continuous improvement, or building quality at every step, depends on everyone's knowledge, and everyone's ability to decide.

More typically, corporate strategies in the food products industry aim for longer shelf life, better margins, and easier shippability. Not health. Not real quality, not at all. These companies' visions center on how much money they can make by driving down the costs of doing business and selling more things quicker. Money goes into advertising to the lowest common denominator, not the kind of nutritional value analysis and quality control that will benefit both consumers and employees. A lot of the big companies sold many deliberately unhealthy products that valued taste and sweetness over nutritional value.

In the last couple of decades, however, we've seen employees and consumers swing back. If you worked for a company that sold the kind of low-quality food that's filled with additives, sugars, and dyes, maybe you wouldn't be so proud to go home and tell your community what you did for a living. No one wants to say, "Hey, you know, I'm the head manager responsible for production at the poison company." You'd probably be halfway out the door the whole time. Maybe that's why the same companies are acquiring natural and organic product lines, and they're trying to change because they *have to* change.

More employees *want* to be proud of the products that they're selling. More consumers and employees *want* to make this world a healthier place.

There's no longer such a solid line between good and bad, though.

When we were starting up, marketers created a lot of poorly thought-out products and didn't reflect on what the negative outcomes might be on people's health. But consumers became trapped in a cycle of buying what was marketed to them. And that simply doesn't work in the world we're experiencing right now. What's poorly thought-out is easily rooted out, and social media is there to shame anyone who doesn't do right by others.

This is right where **founder-product-market fit** comes into play.

- A lot of businesses, if not most businesses, focus on the framework of **product-market fit,** which is the idea that you can basically copycat or build upon an existing product idea and shift it into a different or larger market. Let's use a silly example. Most companies think that if people like tofu in Ireland, they're definitely going to like tofu in the United States. It's a calculated approach to making money. Knowing your product and market is important, but it's not the only thing that matters.

- Instead, I like to shift the people I mentor toward **founder-product fit.** Why is the founder interested in this product, and are they a natural fit to leading this product forward? Can they carry this brand? Are they going to do *anything* necessary to make this vision a reality? And if they aren't interested, how are they going to convince their employees to be interested as well?

- But then, even more so, there's the importance of **founder-market fit**. If you're a vegan consumer, you're not going to be starting a meat snack brand, right? If you want to get into the natural health industry and really don't understand the consumer, why are you even thinking about it? Do you understand why someone would be vegetarian? Do you care about people who are sensitive to allergens? Do you want to talk to those folks and become their friends?

Bringing it all together into an ideal **founder-product-market fit** is the best-case scenario.

Even so, entrepreneurs often have shiny-object syndrome, the kind of narrow vision that doesn't allow them to ask the right questions about their own intentions and fit. I hear about it all the time. "Since people like red, white, and blue in the United States, the company should sell red, white, and blue tofu there because it will be *that much more* popular! We'll make a fortune!" It doesn't really work that way most of the time!

In fact, if a product represents true innovation, then focusing only on product-market fit is going to require thorough testing and research. It may actually take a lot of time to get that product into stores. But entrepreneurs sometimes think that they can reinvent breakfast cereal and make a ton of money, and they forget about the values, culture, and community that drive true innovation and long-term relationships with customers.

I had a conversation just like this recently with my younger half-brother, Stefano.

"Hey Mike, I want to open a coffee shop. I really like coffee."

"Want to open a coffee shop?" I asked. "Go work at Starbucks for six months and learn how to be a good barista. Learn how to be a good coffee manager. Learn on someone else's dime how world-class does it."

"Really?"

"Really. And then find out if you have a founder-product-market fit. Just because you're interested in coffee doesn't mean it's going to work. You need put your own spin on it."

You can't just step out as a former executive or sales manager and say, "Now's the time I ought to lead my own product line." If you want to create a plant-based chicken company, because we now know that consumers really want plant-based chicken, you have to have a really good reason to jump into that business. Maybe you've been a vegan for a decade and you understand the consumer intimately. Maybe you're a farmer with a wonderful knack for recipe development. If you aren't, you probably don't have a strong enough vision to be in that business.

Please don't believe someone who doesn't believe in you.

I can tell you that there are days when I don't feel like a healthy person, when I don't feel like a successful entrepreneur, when I don't feel like a good mentor. But with the passion I have for my work, I can stay focused on the fundamentals, and that means believing in what I do and in my own vision.

A lot of times we don't do things that matter to us because we're scared of being embarrassed or of being held accountable, or even, on some level, afraid to tell our family and friends that this is something we want to do. Why is it so hard to tell people what we want?

And that's why believing in what I do now means believing in new founders, even when they change their vision mid-stream.

Let's take Three Farmers Foods. Natasha (CEO) and Elysia Vandenhurk (CRO) founded and run the business. They work alongside their cofounders, the literal three farmers in their brand name: their father, Dan Vandenhurk, and his farming neighbors, Colin Rosengren and Ron Emde.

More consumers and employees *want* **to make this world a healthier place.**

When they were just starting out, Three Farmers had a vision of selling crops directly from their farm in Saskatchewan. Their aim was to add more value to their crops. That was their business plan.

But getting their products supported was a bit more complicated than they expected. Camelina seed oil was their first product, followed by chickpeas. But neither of these was a financially sustainable option for a large community of consumers. It just wasn't going to work. A vision like that could be good for running a local community shop along with other farm products, or for targeting direct sales to businesses that needed the oil for their own products. But Three Farmers wasn't likely going to grow outside of that scope if they stayed on that path.

We got to talking about what Natasha and Elysia were actually passionate about. I never nudged; I only asked questions. I believed in their passion and did not want to replace that with any kind of vision of my own.

"We're prairie folk," Natasha told me. "We found our niche in roasted pulse snacks because these incredibly important plants help add nitrogen to the soil, and it just made sense. But it was 2009 when we started looking at this concept of using camelina seed oil, which is normally sold to product manufacturers, as a stepping stone. At the time, we researched the oil and started to understand its properties and why it was different. We saw that consumers were responding to the whole farm-to-fork process as well."

I found out that Elysia was a Red Seal Chef and had worked with many accomplished leaders in food service, including globally renowned chef Susur Lee. Natasha had majored in economics and knew a lot about how agriculture fit into the future of food sustainability.

Growing up in an agricultural community, both women were also passionate about farming and wanted to support their father's homegrown dedication to the land.

Dan's crops were focused on pulses like chickpeas as well as lentils, produce that's high in protein and fiber, low in fats and calories.

What happens when you combine all of these wonderful foods, mixed with the kind of culinary flavors a chef can bring to the table? An absolutely outstanding pulse snacking company.

"We wanted to add transparency and traceability to our food supply, and launch it to the retail landscape around the world," Natasha explained. "But the first thing we needed to find out was what that idea really looked like for us. I didn't want a sugarcoated version of our market; I wanted to have real conversations about what the market was looking for. What are our unique assets? What communities do we belong to? How can we structure our future?"

From Natasha and Elysia's point of view as well as from a consumer standpoint, that's an outstanding vision. The potential is endless and exciting, with consumer demand pointing Three Farmers in a number of new directions to expand their product line.

"What we found out was that people buying natural foods are looking for something accessible, just like any other shopper," Natasha pointed out. "So what we needed to do was address the real challenge in consumer food products, and that's distribution. People need to be able to find the product when they need it—in grocery stores, but also club stores, airports, and online."

Instead of a product-market fit, the Three Farmers team sought out founder-product fit and founder-market fit. When that vision was clear, they were able to create a minimum viable community, namely, the kind of consumer response that allowed them to sell products sustainably. Three Farmers is everywhere now, including grocery stores, drug stores, and even nationwide at high-end chains like Whole Foods. Their community has taken on a life of its own.

And I have been so lucky to watch their transformation into a significant business with a clear vision of where they're going over the next ten years. They've reached the tipping point to success.

As a young entrepreneur at Manitoba Harvest, I had founder-product fit because I lost weight and was interested in health. I didn't have any experience in business, but at least that aspect of the business matched up with what I wanted to see in myself. I had founder-market fit because I cared about seeing other people's health journeys turn positive, just like mine.

Over time, I developed a deeper, richer version of my vision. I discovered founder-product-market fit because I put my whole heart into what I did and I stuck to my vision of a healthier society.

So if you're looking to found your own business, your own vision has to be paramount.

- Remember that you're never an imposter in your own game. What you're passionate about really matters.

- You can Kanban your way through your own business issues. Put a sticky note on sticky problems, and then call on those friendships, ask more questions, and make changes as you go.

- A vision can naturally evolve out of the community and friendships you've already established and allows everyone's passionate ideas to infuse your future success.

- You don't have to replicate old business ideas and models to be successful. Instead, you need to find the founder-product-market fit that works for you.

- Your personal integrity and team integrity are important because they're at the heart of building goodwill with your community.

- Believe in people who believe in you, and send that belief right back out into your community.

LESSON 7
EMPOWER YOUR TEAM

FOR THE longest time, I was only on Team Mom.

I was pissed off that my dad treated my mom badly, and I was pissed off that he didn't take care of us. I didn't regret that our family had split apart when I was two years old. It was probably better that way. I remember waiting for my dad to pick us up on weekends in the Thunder Bay years, and being happy when he didn't show up.

Mom was supportive and I could always count on her. If my mom ever had an issue with me, she just talked about it. She was always in her words.

But after Dad, Mom kind of soured on intimate partner relationships in general. She was very clear that she was done with that kind of relationship for the rest of her life, after the experience she had with my dad. She liked being a mother of two boys. I personally think that her relationship with us was healing. Her trauma eased over time, and although she had a lot of opportunities to find another life partner, nothing came of it. For all of her life, Mom encouraged me and Donny, supported us, and was there with us every step of the way.

When Don and I were in our early twenties, and Manitoba Harvest was just starting to rise, we still had a lot of family in Thunder Bay where Dad lived. We had been visiting him more frequently, trying to get our relationship back on track. Don and I decided to go camping there one summer, and we started thinking back on our early years and about how infrequently we'd seen Dad when we were kids. When we were poor, Mom had worked so hard, and life had been really hard for all of us. We were still both so angry. I was at the point where I had continued my relationship with Dad, but I was old enough to really understand what had gone on between my parents. A lot had been hidden from us, on purpose. And Dad was to blame.

In the wee hours of the morning, Donny and I were drinking wine by the campfire.

"I think we should just... I don't know. Beat him up or something. I don't know, but I feel like I have to do something," I said.

"What, you mean like fully dragging him in the bush and beating him up or whatever?" Donny asked me.

"I don't know. Yes?"

Don nodded. "Seriously, I get where you're going with this. It's not like he doesn't deserve what's coming to him."

The next day, we were still convinced we had to do something. We just had to. It was too much to hold, this feeling of overwhelming sadness about the beginning of our lives, this total loss of a father figure when I was only two years old. The impact on Mom. Her constant drive to work to put food on the table. The way we saw ourselves, the way we valued ourselves, all connected back to the choices that Dad made.

So we went over to talk to Dad: Don, Don's business partner (who was also one of my best friends), and me, not knowing what was going to happen next.

Dad sat down with us, one of his own friends at his side, and he started talking. He talked about how hard times were when he lived in Italy as a child, when he was four or five years old and there was no food. He told us how he went to school only until third grade because he had to start working for a living. Growing up, he had only known desperation.

And I was honest as well. When he left, it broke my heart. It was the first time I remember really coming out and speaking my mind to him.

All five of us were bawling our eyes out for probably an hour, and then there was a moment of connection. Our relationship totally changed from that day on. From that day, he *really* became my dad. We meet up two or three times a year. We have a bond. We spend time in Italy together, having a true relationship across our extended family. He got married again, and I have a half-brother and half-sister.

I learned a lot from that moment with my dad, from the emotional release and relief that followed. Most of all, I learned how to use my words, something that my mom had taught me but that had never sunk in until I addressed that shared trauma.

That moment created a new playing field for me, not just in my personal life but also in how I decided to interact with the world, my business partners, and especially my team. That day, I learned that to actually make that moment of connection, you have to be open, and to be open, you have to listen. It was a lesson that showed me something important that could be applied in all aspects of my life: The essence of the most effective kind of leadership starts with connection. One moment of connection opens all doors. One moment of connection allows for changes to emerge that I might never have thought possible. One moment of connection means that we can all be on the same level playing field.

I believe in servant leadership.

Robert Greenleaf, who wrote *The Power of Servant-Leadership*, famously said, "The only test of leadership is that somebody follows—voluntarily." An example of the power of servant leadership is demonstrated in the abolition of slavery among

The essence
of the most
effective kind
of leadership
**starts with
connection.**

the Religious Society of Friends—the American Quaker movement—led by John Woolman. In his book, Greenleaf explains that, by 1770, almost a hundred years before the rest of the United States change their laws, no Quakers held slaves. Woolman convinced people in his community to give up their slaves, one at a time, through dialogue and leading by example. Such small steps can lead to big ideas, and big changes in how we do things.

For me, servant leadership means that I listen first—*before* I lead, *before* I help my team put their great ideas into action.

Sure, I believe in servant leadership from a soul standpoint. But I've also learned a lot as a leader from mentors and great leaders in the field, whether they're a part of a team sport or organization or political governance. And what I've found is that being a good leader is about doing the right things so people want to follow you.

To start, I set a rule for success, and that is to always lead by example. Countless times over the years, I repeated what I learned from the examples of my own mentors, and I just got better and better at practicing those examples. I always want to walk a mile in the shoes of the people who've mentored me, or whom I hire in any role. I want to truly see how things work for each person. In trying on roles for myself, I can have a realistic understanding of what challenges each of my team members faces, and what they need to do to be successful at accomplishing their tasks. Only then can I empower each team member to build toward that success.

But let's take a step back for a second. Even in big companies, it's typical to have either a front-of-house or back-of-house kind of CEO, and the former is the most prevalent because sales and marketing are primary to entrepreneurship. In some ways, I'm fairly unique as an entrepreneur because I'm primarily a finance person. From being at my mom's side during her accounting work, I learned very early in life that numbers and formulas are very easy for me. This has helped me operationally, in the back end of the business, to engineer manufacturing processes and land contracts that allow the company to build revenue.

And because of my lifestyle and focus on understanding our customers, I've developed some of those needed sales and marketing strengths over time.

This doesn't mean that I'm a sales and marketing expert, though. It means I'm genuinely interested in these parts of the business. But they're not my go-to.

As entrepreneurs, founders have to be able to do that internal assessment. What are you really good at, and where can you learn?

But the reality is that no one has to learn it all, and especially not founders. The friendships and communities you create can help bolster you and your ideas, but what you really need is to be able to rely on a team of people who are just as skilled as you are, only in a wide variety of ways. For me, the values that have driven Manitoba Harvest's culture have always been linked to empowerment.

A Culture of Empowerment

So, what does a culture of empowerment really look like?

1   **Every day and every meeting should start with listening.**
    My personal life journey means that I've learned how to hold space for difficult conversations, and to put people at ease when they come to me with a challenge. Listening is the fastest way to walk a mile in someone else's shoes.

2   **Founders have to have enough self-awareness to be able
to say, "This is where I need help."** Micromanagement
has to end. Period. As a founder, you don't have to come
equipped with all the answers, and there's a reason you've
hired people to help you out. Trust them and their individual
expertise. Don't let your ego take over, trying to solve every
problem.

3   **Always remember that there is no one right answer.**
Looking at yourself and your passion, and understanding
what your own skill set is, what your own competencies are,
is important. But what has to guide you is a combination of
those instincts and what the business needs, and your team
has to provide multiple lenses on those needs.

4   **Create an environment of openness.** Founders do their
best when they're connecting people and ideas, bridging
the gaps for community, and allowing equality to be front
and center.

A culture of empowerment means hiring for empowerment.

You need a team with competencies, for sure, not only in the
key roles for each position but also competencies in the core
values of the business. The more refined your core values are,
the easier it is to seek out the right people for the roles you
need to fill.

In the previous chapter, I talked a lot about Manitoba Harvest's core value of quality. But there were five other values
that also drove our business and our success. These are:

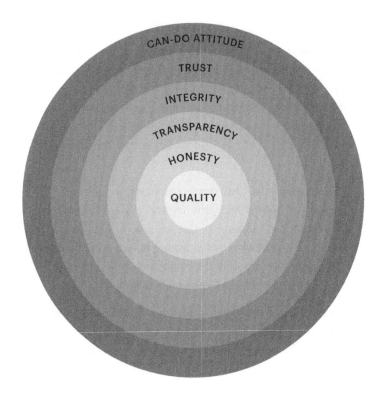

How does this all come together?

If we're talking about our value of *quality*, for example, then I'd say that the most important role at Manitoba Harvest was our janitorial and sanitation team. If the place wasn't clean, we were out of business. Because we were in the food business. So, walking a mile in a janitor's shoes, I would have to explore what would make it easiest for that person to connect with the Toyota method. I would want to make sure that they had the ability to speak up often and always. But I've also found that *trust* and innovation are clearly linked, because we have to be able to trust ourselves to try and implement something new, bold, and different from the same old thing we've seen on grocery shelves. Even more so, trust in all directions is a lost art that ought to count more in our modern world because of the way it empowers us individually and together. *Honesty*, *transparency*, and *integrity* allow us to make decisions that are both ethical and achievable, and a *can-do attitude* makes it all happen effectively.

That's why setting up an empowerment-based culture instead of the typical hierarchical approach was so critical to our success. If I didn't make sure, right from the beginning, that every hire felt as though they could speak up, I would have failed at serving Manitoba Harvest's best interests.

When I look at hiring now, I put together competency-based questions that match the position description and what we need that person to do. That rolls into a checklist audit scoresheet. But I focus my real attention on the feelings I get hanging out with that person, and the confidence I get in their values fit. Then I check my feelings out in discussions with other members of the team.

I rely on a quantitative *and* qualitative analysis of each individual.

The flipped triangle is where you want to go.

There was a time when I declared war on the word "employee." That word wouldn't be uttered at Manitoba Harvest, I had said to my team. It won't be on any of our documentation, wouldn't be a part of the employment equation at all.

It was an idea I learned about from Whole Foods Market, where they have teams and team members, not managers and employees. And so we changed every HR document, every file in the business, over the course of six months. We created the foundation of teamwork first and foremost.

I say "foundation" specifically: this word relates to giving people opportunities to shine and grow through mistakes, and really evolve in the business. A team environment is much better, much more conducive to business evolution, than an owner-oriented environment where there's one boss and direction comes only from the top.

Servant leadership isn't shared leadership. It's the recognition that founders and so-called senior members of the team are *actually serving everyone else*.

I'm not exaggerating. If you're deciding what to do with your revenue, you've got to serve the organization first.

This leads me to what I really want you to take away from this chapter: your organizational chart needs to look like a flipped triangle, where the bulk of your team members are at the top.

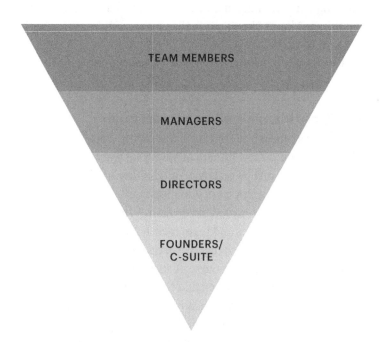

TEAM MEMBERS

MANAGERS

DIRECTORS

FOUNDERS/
C-SUITE

What do you need to be successful? Not a CEO. You need team members. *Team members are the most critical part of the whole organization.* The people who used to be at the top of the triangle—the C-suite, the directors, and so on? They are the support system. They exist only to make sure the rest of the team is given the resources they need to get their jobs done effectively.

Let's think about cooking a meal for your best friend. At home, if you're trying to cook but the whole kitchen is messy, you might realize that the most important thing to do first is clean up and set the stage so you can make a meal more easily. Maybe you could wash dishes after you use them instead of waiting for all of them to pile up. You don't just make a meal on top of a pile of dirty pots and pans. And if you're following a recipe, perhaps you're missing an ingredient you forgot to pick up at the store.

No matter what, if you want your meal for your best friend to be successful, you assess what's needed, shift your perspective, make intelligent substitutions, and do the dirty work. There's no one there to do all those tasks for you while you wait to jump in at the last second and get all of the credit. What's important to getting the meal made isn't just the recipe or the end result—it's all the tasks, best practices, and tools you need to make it happen successfully.

The same thing is true in business.

- When we place our people at the bottom, we disregard not only their value in getting tasks done but also the insight they have on how to get tasks done *better*.

- When we place our people at the bottom, we often take credit for their hard work, which minimizes their self-worth and value and decreases the meaning in their work.

- When we place our people at the bottom, we lose track of what's really important: friendship, community, mentorship, and shared experiences.

It can be a challenge to get there, to get to true servant leadership as an entrepreneur and founder.

That's because almost all of us start off as a team of one. When we start hiring people, that owner-operator mentality is just the norm, and it's hard to shift. When the business transitions to raising money and capital, and shareholders and other stakeholders, like a board of directors, start walking in the door, a lot more structure is needed. At that point in the organization's evolution, it can be a challenge for the founder to transition to a different mindset.

Now, I'm on Team Team.

The biggest barrier to change is a stuck mindset, characterized by phrases like, "that's just how it's done," "best practices," "them's the rules," "that's what I was told." Most of us hear these phrases every day, from our parents, children, workmates, bosses. We all know why they exist and why we use them. There are many rules in our day-to-day existence, from the rules of how to dress for work, to the rules of doing our jobs, to the rules of being successful.

The social culture that replicates old rules also demands what we're supposed to be if we're leaders. What we think leadership means is very entrenched in our social norms. In fact, what we believe about leadership isn't too far removed from what we believe about old-school parenting: Someone's in charge. Someone should be seen and not heard. No one should question the people at the top of the ladder.

But old-school best practices don't always work in the present day. And if they do, there is nothing to say that "best" lasts,

Team members are the most critical part of **the whole organization.**

either. In today's workplaces, older leadership paradigms are working less powerfully than they have in the past because they've made our places of work rigid rather than adaptable. Just as the rules of parenting have shifted, so should our understanding of leadership.

I grew up with a mom who talked to me like I mattered. Who listened to me. Who let me try to do things the way I knew worked for me. Maybe she let me do it my way because I was headstrong, or maybe she could see me struggling to fit in. Maybe part of the reason she let me explore outside the lines was that she wanted to see a future for me that didn't replicate the past, the difficulties she faced trying to fit into the box that society had built for a woman born in the 1950s. But most of all, she put herself at the bottom of that triangle and provided me with the resources I needed to succeed.

When Donny and I sat down with our dad, we listened. He listened. And then, by offering up that opportunity to listen on both sides, we changed the way *we connected*.

Parents of all kinds do things differently these days, and the hierarchy most families used to have is eroding. Parents are listening more. They're adapting to their kids' personalities and unique identities. Like my own mom, modern parents exist to help their kids physically, socially, and emotionally. That doesn't mean that parents don't have a leadership role in their families, but their leadership comes from the intrinsic knowing and love they offer up to each person they mentor.

In business, there are parallels. Clearly, the idea of a leader as a corporate parent shouldn't even come into the equation when it comes to building an organizational structure. Even so, in a similar way to how parenthood has changed, our sense of hierarchy at work also has to change.

Founders and other leaders need to let go of the idea that they magically know better than other skilled, experienced, and educated adults *all the time*.

What if we realized, once and for all, that being at the top of the ladder didn't actually matter at the end of the day? What if we stopped assuming that everyone else was also reaching toward the top and that we had to compete? Because in our new, Great Resignation, quiet-quitting work dynamic, that just isn't always true. What if we also realized that the old rules for leadership, work, and life are just bad habits, dying systems, or crappy work-culture norms, and we can call these what they are? What if we could change them? Can we give ourselves permission to actually say it like it is and make different choices?

We're all on the same team. Leaders included. And we're all here to listen, to learn, and to support each other's amazing work.

LESSON 8
IT TAKES A NATION

UNTIL YOUR consumer packaged goods company reaches around a million dollars in sales per year, you could go under almost any day.

I mean, of course, every business is different. You're not likely going to need a million dollars to run a naturopathy office or a handmade furniture studio for the long haul.

But the premise is the same for all businesses: you have to reach for a minimum viable community that will keep your business going. You need enough money coming in the door every day that you'll be able to pay your bills, employ your team, and invest in honing your business ideas, products, and services.

When we first started the business, I used to think, almost daily: "Are we going to make it tomorrow? Are we going to make it next week?"

The business was growing, but were we actually creating success? There were a million hard times, hard decisions, way before there was a million dollars. There were so many times when, as an entrepreneur, I felt frustrated and wanted to give up, or the obstacle in front of us seemed so insurmountable that it would destroy us, or that we'd have to die trying. And then I would panic: If we didn't have this business, where would I get my hemp foods from personally?

It was the personal stories that kept me going when I felt overwhelmed. The testimonials started coming during the first month already, and we didn't even have to ask for them. Senior citizens were saying they had started taking hemp oil or eating Hemp Hearts, our fastest-growing product, and the arthritis in their wrists was disappearing. They were feeling better than they had in years. So much anecdotal evidence was coming in, and whether or not these health results were directly tied to Hemp Hearts, that just fired me up.

I realized that what I had in front of me was a bigger mission than I had expected. It was bigger than me and my own health journey. It was bigger than the cofounders and their personal goals. It was bigger than our team.

"This is a movement, so we have to keep going," I said to myself. "You don't have an option to back out now."

It took five years to get that first million dollars in sales for Manitoba Harvest. The first year we were in business, 1998, we reached $50,000 in sales. It felt like a lot. Not enough for we three founders to quit our day jobs, but enough to feel good about what we were trying to make real. By 2003, we were at about a million dollars in sales. Five years later, at year ten, we reached $10 million.

We rolled everything back into capitalizing the business and expanding manufacturing and farming operations. Everything was growing as we were, and we became a vertically integrated company. From researching the genetics of our hemp, to getting seed to the farmers, to buying the grain back, and then operating the manufacturing process as well as the brand's development, it was all-encompassing.

With venture capital coming in the door in around 2009, it was a whole different story. We were coming to the end of one business life cycle and starting another. My cofounders left the business a few years after the venture capital investment because they felt it was time for them to move in a different direction.

By 2014, Manitoba Harvest reached $50 million in sales. We took on institutional investors and formed a proper board of directors and governance structure. And then things really started to pick up.

We had a billion-dollar private equity sponsor on board and sold a majority share to them. A few months after the ink dried on that sale process, with the support of our private equity partner we acquired a friend's company, our biggest competitor. The friend and I had known each other for over two decades, and we had parallel businesses: while Manitoba Harvest focused on our public brand name and had secured 15,000 retail partners, including every major grocery store, my friend's company focused on selling industrial ingredients to other manufacturers, which they in turn used for cereals and bars and other products. But a $42 million transaction meant that Manitoba Harvest had acquired two manufacturing facilities, and we were ready to support that movement.

It was a massive win for all of us. Our community had become a nation. And our nation needed us to show up to work in a whole different way.

If it takes a village to raise a family, it takes a nation to raise an entrepreneur.

Imposter syndrome affected me a lot as we grew as a company because of where I came from personally. My background did not set me up for absolute confidence.

To me, imposter syndrome relates a lot to our social and cultural norms. As I explained in the last chapter, leadership is almost always associated with willful, individualistic, and hierarchical values, and I know I never fit into those ways of operating. But there's also a more popular version of a CEO, one that's grounded in media values, one with sharp suits, a trust fund, and a Harvard MBA. I'm not that person, either. I

It's not work hard, play hard.

It's passion first, work second.

didn't have the right background or the money or the social ties that many other business leaders had. I definitely didn't want to put on a suit. So, for much of the time when I was starting out in business, I felt as if I didn't align with a lot of people's expectations, and it wasn't a comfortable place to be in.

The more I've grown as an individual and in business, however, the more I've become comfortable with myself—just being me—so that I have been able to make the impact I want to make. And the more impactful I am, the more community I have around me. The more community I have around me, the more people who want me to win and to be part of it.

But first I had to challenge those societal norms that triggered my imposter syndrome in the first place. Entrepreneurship was quickly becoming a holistic lifestyle for me. Of course, with the benefit of youth when I was weight training five to six times a week, I actually had the stamina to keep going on pure adrenaline. I was able to stave off the worst of imposter syndrome by just working harder and longer. But that's not sustainable. It's also not realistic for many people with great ideas who have children to raise, or grandparents to take care of, or siblings to shelter. It's not realistic, as well, to work in a world where overtime and overwork are constant.

We don't have to be imposters, though, to be leaders. We don't have to and we shouldn't have to pretend to be people we're not. Because that doesn't really line up with having your best day ever. I found out that I could run a company and still show up in a baseball cap and T-shirt, but, even more importantly, in doing so I could still be speaking as my true self and upholding the values of the kind of business I wanted to thrive in.

I think more than ever we're living in a time when, because of storytelling online, in the media, society is interested in who we authentically are. The same is true for entrepreneurship.

Whether you have a weight loss story or lifestyle change like the kind I experienced or embody a spiritual or motivational moment that turned into your business, people want to hear about it. And it allows you that bit of freedom you need to take steps forward.

Even later in life, when it comes to entrepreneurship, there's a different set of stakes that can lead to imposter syndrome. Once you've established yourself, you're holding that vision of the company and you feel a great deal of responsibility to all of your stakeholders. There is no turning it off. Especially nowadays, nonstop email communications and texts mean that you're staying up to the moment on information about your business and your competitors in the industry whether you like it or not. But when you recognize the role of meaning-making in your work, you can look at that lifestyle differently.

It's not work hard, play hard. It's passion first, work second.

Growing up in Hamilton, Ontario, Margaret Coons started eating a plant-based diet when she was twelve years old. When she was old enough to start making her own meals, Margaret spent a lot of time looking for protein alternatives, especially when it came to cheese.

"Everything I could find was that plastic shredded cheese that you used to see," she told me. "Primarily processed products that don't make you feel good, that don't taste good."

That lack of flavor is what inspired her to get into the culinary arts and open her own vegan business, experimenting with nut-based cheeses.

"Working at a restaurant, I really honed my recipe for vegan cheese," she told me. "And, you know, I didn't really have a plan other than to maybe sell the cheese to plant-based restaurants, but then I decided I was going to try farmers markets. I was talking to people and handing out samples, and Nuts for Cheese became very popular. Suddenly, I had to learn quickly how to pack up bulk cheese, I had to learn about labeling requirements, and I was making products at restaurants in the middle of the night to meet demand."

I met Margaret soon after she started promoting her brand at a launchpad competition, where I was a judge. Nuts for Cheese won an award for the most innovative new product, for good reason, and we stayed in touch. Mentoring Margaret and her team made sense because there were a lot of parallels between what she was trying to do and what I did at Manitoba Harvest.

"You know, when you're growing a manufacturing company from a start-up, there are a few barriers to leveling up," she said. "I was renting a restaurant when I started, but it made more sense to become a manufacturer, and those are two very different types of organizations. It's exactly the point when you have to think about raising money. That's also the time when you need a professional board. We needed to raise a million dollars for the company so we could expand across North America and manage our business growth trajectory."

But raising investor capital doesn't mean that you have to give up what you believe in doing. For Margaret, and for me, it kind of means the opposite.

"If you're passionate," Margaret said, "you have to show up for yourself. If you are considering starting a company, it has to be about that passion because it's hard and it requires a lot of attention and sacrifice. Commitment. I think you have to have the vision to see something through, and you have to structure that challenge to make sure that *you* are effective first."

As Margaret says, it's critical for founders to understand what happens when you make that leap from entrepreneur to CEO. At Manitoba Harvest, when we got past that $10 million mark, that's when I made my own leap.

Ten years in, I found out that being an entrepreneur and being a CEO are two totally different things. For me, bringing venture capital into the mix at Manitoba Harvest was a big part of that transition, because it meant that we had to report to people other than, well, us. And we had to prove our business case in order to get the capital to create our nation.

It was like going from the junior leagues to the major leagues.

At the time, I felt pride, accomplishment. Although I knew that the new league I was playing in was just that much harder, and it was going to require both personal growth and refinement of lifestyle and routine in order to be successful, I also knew that the benefits would be outstanding. Making the leap to CEO allowed me to fully embrace my own continuous improvement as a new lifestyle and mindset.

Remember, business works in exactly the same way as people do on their own. That's because businesses are made up of people.

Many CEOs like to try out so-called best practices on how to plan for the future of their business, and where to put their resources so that they can maximize revenue, but that jump in revenue generation just doesn't *happen*.

Instead, what happens is finding balance. When I first took the leap, I wasn't always balanced. I thought that I had to handle the situation, and I didn't have an intuitive feeling about what to do or the benefit of the wisdom I have now. I was looking for examples of other CEOs who made the leap before me. And I knew that nutrition and diet and exercise from my lifestyle changes made me feel good. So I just started to put a new routine together, aiming for a peak performance kind of mindset, but it was more about having a highest-quality approach to my own core values.

For me, when I became a CEO, I realized that I could not change who I was for anyone, unless my nation wanted me to

It's about bringing everyone out to play and knowing they're right there with you, **and being that support system for them.**

change. But in my industry, my integrity stood for something, and even with an influx of investors, I had to stay strong in my conviction to be myself and support the same values I had always had, no matter what.

What coming to this point in our journey did make us realize, however, was that our minimum viable community required us to become *really* accessible. For Manitoba Harvest, one of the things we had to do to keep meeting our community's needs was to have our most innovative, bestselling product, Hemp Hearts, absolutely everywhere. People were using it daily, even at every meal. From food stores to corner stores, in massive Costco-size packaging to a tiny pocket pack that could fit in someone's purse, Hemp Hearts needed to be available all over so that it could align with the kind of lifestyle choices that our work had inspired in our customers. But we also had to keep talking to people everywhere—consumer shows, online, and in stores—to make sure we weren't missing out on their next request of us.

But our approach is not going to be your approach. We just learned to understand where and when our nation wanted to come together.

The idea of building a nation is expansive, not expensive.

Even as a CEO, your job is to ensure that you're creating the capacity to keep being passionate about what you do every day so that you can keep getting something out of the work that has meaning to you. Building a minimum viable community isn't just about hitting those financial goals, it's about bringing everyone out to play and knowing they're right there with you, and being that support system for them.

It's servant leadership times a million.

Meaning-making as a CEO can still feel like play, however, if it has substance. It's a little like the difference between the kind of food I ate as a child and the meals I make for my family now. Spending five minutes at a drive-through might fill your stomach, but it's nothing like spending the whole day making an authentic Italian tomato sauce inspired by trips to my dad's home country and spending time with family. It feels amazing to tap into the kind of culture, history, family, connection, and food that is not only healthy but also delicious. It feels amazing to feed my kids and have them taste their family's handed-down skills and memories. They'll never remember that drive-through. They are going to remember being surrounded by love.

If you're an entrepreneur who shifts into CEO mode, you have to make sure that you enjoy the journey *more* than anyone else.

It's not a forty-hour week. It's not a sixty-hour week. It's more like 168 hours a week.

So you'd better love what you do, and make sure you've got that nation surrounding you, so that your business is 100 percent sustainable.

I lead from my heart, and when I have a community behind me, I feel unstoppable.

It's how we feel when we build outward that makes a true difference. We are stronger together!

As you move into a bigger role with responsibilities, ask yourself what you need to support your new nation.

- What's the minimum viable community of people who support my business that I need to build?

- What am I doing to get those people on board?

- How long is it going to take to prove my bigger-business model?

- What are the resources I need to keep going?

- Whom do I need by my side?

- What am I doing to support my nation once I hit my community-building goal?

You want to start close to home and get your footing first. Many people in the health products industry want to get their products on the shelves of Whole Foods or Safeway right away so they can nail that minimum viable community fast. But what you *should* be able to do immediately is sell your product up and down your own street. Especially with a lot of sales online nowadays, you can develop your minimum viable community in the lowest-cost ways so that you can achieve your first steps on a small business budget over the first eighteen to twenty-four months.

You don't have to move fast. You have to make your nation last.

That's because even if you're a CEO, it doesn't have to be you against the world. You can also find others who can mentor you, and you can find that your nation might just be ready to leap alongside you. We can fulfill our needs and build a bigger place for all of us to succeed if we learn how to mutually support each other.

In aiming for supporting a minimum viable community, you're not just stopping at building a group of like-minded people. You're reaching out to expand the idea of what it means to make life better for more people, every day. And you can rise to the occasion, standing up for what you believe in every step of the way.

No compromises.

LESSON 9
EXIT
STAGE YOU

JUST AS I reached my highest level of financial success, I hit my personal rock bottom.

The mother of my children and I decided to separate on February 3, 2019. We had gone to Costa Rica a couple of weeks earlier to try and bond, to save our marriage, to reconnect. Even though it would require supporting our family through a lot of hard changes, we both returned home clear on the fact that we were in a new phase, one where co-parenting was our focus. Less than two weeks later, on Valentine's Day, my partners and I announced that we were selling the business. We knew the business sale process was going through, but with my divorce on the horizon, our team took a couple of weeks to regroup before making the sale details public. And it was just then that, as I mentioned in the first chapter of this book, my mother suddenly passed away.

All of this, this triple grieving loss, happened within eight weeks. It was almost unbearable for me.

In the eighteen months before I left Manitoba Harvest, the passion I'd had for the business I had created was eroding, much to my surprise. The practical realities of dealing with private equity strategies had left me exhausted, but it seemed to be more than that. Everything I had built still mattered, but there were fewer and fewer best days. I was feeling overwhelmed and the path that I needed to follow didn't light up before me as it had in the past. Worst of all, I didn't have the mental space to repair what was broken.

Even before my relationship ended and my mom passed away, I knew I needed some time to myself, which is why I decided that it might be a good idea to hire a different CEO. As a vertically integrated business with about $100 million in annual revenue, we had a massive number of hemp industry assets, and there was a lot to do in planning our next phase. I was still around, but I made a hard decision, one that meant I was no longer an executive helping steer the company. I retreated to the board as a director and shareholder.

By February 2019, on the brink of my successive personal disasters, we decided to sell the company to global hemp industry giant Tilray for $419 million.

On paper, it sounds amazing. But given what happened next, it didn't feel as good as it should have. Selling the business didn't provide me with that essential feeling of relief I had expected.

When we are grieving, there's a tendency for us to focus on our pain and our inability to move in any direction. It is all-encompassing, that sense that life has gone still, has frozen, because without our loved ones beside us, what point is there in trying? The worst part is that if we try to get out of the cycle of grief without resolving it, we're going to become one of the worst versions of ourselves. Trying to shy away from that pain and build up emotional barriers to it is going to impact, successively, every relationship that we have in our lives. Just when we need people the most, we're not going to get the support we need to heal.

The first therapy session I went to was for couples therapy with my then wife. The therapist, who became my personal counselor and has been helping me for ten years now, asked me a really hard question right out of the gate.

"Tell me an example of what love looks like," she asked.

I couldn't talk. I actually experienced a deep emotional response, complete with a full, convulsive kind of crying for twenty minutes, sitting on her couch with my wife.

"Well, that triggered something, I think," I said when I could finally speak.

The therapist nodded. "What are you trying to create in a couple's relationship? Maybe let's start there?"

"What do I know about what a good relationship looks like?" was my response. "My dad and mom broke up, and I was generally abandoned by my dad. I mean, I just want to have a consistent relationship and stuff like that."

"But working through those things and being honest about them," the therapist went on to say, "means that you have the potential to come out on the other side. That's not a weakness. That's a strength."

I am a bit worn, bruised, and scarred, but I wouldn't want it any other way.

We're feeling beings who think, not thinking beings who feel.

Until my triple grieving loss, I had spent a lot of time working on my physical best self. And it's not that I was disconnected from my emotional self. I had spent a lot of time deliberately creating psychological safety for my team at work, and I believed in personal openness. I had even taken the time, at work especially, to make it very clear that I didn't believe in faking it until you make it. Putting a gloss on who we are as human beings, pretending to be something we're not, just creates barriers to getting the support we authentically need.

So, on one level I believed in the need for emotional health, but on another, I wasn't walking that talk. I had never actually taken a look at how my childhood trauma was still affecting

We need to change the way we think about mental health, **both at home and in the workplace.**

me and even sometimes affecting the way I interacted with others. I wasn't the embodiment of mindful action that I wanted myself to be.

We need to change the way we think about mental health, both at home and in the workplace.

Going to the gym, you can work those muscles out, and that's been a big part of health for me. But going to the therapist to work out our emotions ... well, not all of us are there yet.

In fact, very few of us realize how important emotions are, even in a practical sense. Decades of research on individuals who have had an acute ischemic stroke, for example, show that human beings are all *incapable* of separating their emotions from their decisions. In fact, we need our emotions to make the simplest daily decisions *because we use our feelings to tell us what matters to us.* When we lose the ability to use emotions because of a serious brain injury that affects the parts of our brain that process emotion, we may find it impossible to make even the simplest decisions. People with this condition may not be able to decide what socks to put on in the morning, even if they are given a finite choice between two different options. We use our emotions so consistently and frequently that they are inseparable from our ability to operate in the world.

Knowing this, and having lived through emotions that have left me frozen, I have learned to have more empathy and patience. If someone is having a bad day, we'll do something about it. I'm quick to share not only my personal learnings about the power of emotion but also what I've seen work for other people.

Empathy is the ability to sense where the people on the other side of the table are at, and what bothers them, and recognize their needs. It's also your ability to recognize your own needs. What I've learned by facing my emotions in therapy is that when you share about yourself and your story, it helps you, but it also has the potential to help other people.

How can you increase empathy for yourself and others?

Start with yourself. We always have to take care of ourselves first because that's how we can more easily take care of others. If you can't see yourself taking care of others' emotions, ask yourself what you need to do to get there by taking your intuitive temperature:

- Where am I right now in terms of my emotional expertise?

- Where do I want to be emotionally?

- What's the first thing I can do to get to the root of the problem?

- What can I trust about what I know? If nothing changed from right now until the end of my days, would I be satisfied with how I feel?

- What might I need to push myself forward to find out my next step? Does that need include a therapist?

Every day, create your own opportunities for emotional learning experiences by prioritizing your feelings and emotions and reflecting on them. What comes up for you emotionally in your conversations with others? When you're taking the time to reflect on your own? What feels good and what doesn't? Pay attention to the cues.

Encourage and strive for direct communication at home and work. Actively encourage everyone around you to feel open and honest in your relationships, and do the same in return so you can build mutual connection and compassion.

At work, encourage your team members to define their own boundaries through listening and setting up what works for them. It's okay to say no. By learning to put boundaries in place, you respect yourself and others.

Try to understand what your gut feeling is telling you. If you feel that a part of you is scared, try to understand why. Are you scared because making a decision will push you out of your comfort zone? Or is a red light telling you that something is not right about this decision?

Be loyal to your own thoughts and feelings. We often embrace belief systems that are not ours and live according to them, instead of living according to our own values. Walk the talk, and act according to your values.

Allow your mistakes to be honored. They are legitimate learning opportunities, so don't give yourself a hard time about them.

Don't try to do the many, many things required to get to your emotional peak right away, especially without a therapist in the room. Just start with exploring one thing that comes up for you.

I am a big believer in the idea that this world is not happening *to* us. *We* are happening to the world.

When I left Manitoba Harvest for good, I started to move my way into mentorship as my new purpose. I wanted to help other founders find their way just a little bit easier than I had. I wanted to share what I had discovered and make the path that much clearer for those coming next in the natural products industry.

Just as I had done when I first got started, I began to create a new community. I found that I could offer a thirty-minute strategy chat. I could get entrepreneurs really on their way with a ninety-minute business tune-up, which I think of as being like an oil change. I can get into strategic planning sessions, which traditionally last three or four hours, and really get under the hood and help them lay out a solid year-long plan.

But what I've realized is that I've shifted from coming into these mentoring talks with all of the answers toward allowing the answers to reveal themselves through authentic, psychologically safe conversations.

Here's why. Emerging from my triple grieving loss, I was having even more challenging imposter syndrome feelings than ever. Who was I to tell new founders and entrepreneurs what's going on?

"Wait a sec," I thought. "Instead of teaching new founders, I'm just going to show up and *understand*. I'm going to truly understand and put enough learning into understanding where I believe they are on their path, and then simply tell them what I would do if I was in their situation. I'm not telling them what to do or when."

It's been hugely helpful to recognize how to show up as myself, and to give myself permission to feel okay about it.

To show up in a way that can actually help other people and mentor them in a successful way, I have to have three things:

1   **Authenticity** is the ability to dare to stick to our values and perceptions and act according to them based on our own truth. It's about daring to be in disagreement with people, with kindness. It's about not trying to please others just in order to avoid conflict. When I show up authentically to vet founders' ideas, I can say both yes and no with confidence.

2   **Vulnerability** is when we can express what we think and feel in our own voices, even in situations where we're unsure about the right thing to do next. When I remember that I don't need to know all the answers, I can get into a better flow with the people I mentor.

3   **Reflection** is taking time after an interaction to check in with the ideas presented to me and by me. For me, reflection results in more innovation and the possibility of breakthrough ideas that are truly disruptive, not just

Instead of teaching, just **show up and** *understand.*

cannibalizations of existing product and service lines. Not everything has to be decided at once. I can take the time I need to do a gut check on my first reaction and come back to the table.

The human experience, and all of the emotions we have, should be honored in business.

We need to give our people, our teams, a range of opportunities to listen to each other's stories. As a mentor, I am a student of the human experience, and I rely fully on my own emotions to make decisions that can help others.

Mentoring others, and any kind of emotionally informed business, requires practice. What does this look like? See your own metaphorical reflection. Are you a person people go to when they're facing a challenge? If the answer isn't yes, then know that building your employee community or family or friend group starts with the mirror. Are you a person you would want to work for? Reflect on the hard truth of who you are and who you want to be. It's okay if you're not there yet. It's okay to make a mistake. But it isn't okay to regret.

Where we are right now is a result of the decisions we've made that got us here. Today is a new opportunity to make a different set of choices. After all, today is all we have. Right now is all we have. Right now is exactly where we need to be.

Right now is an opportunity we can take on as a challenge if we want it to be. We can go into the gutter or off the rails or right down that path to success. We can choose. We have to think deeply about whether a challenge we are dealing with is actually *true or not*, and if it's possible for us to imagine our lives without that challenge. The emotional work we all have to do in our lives to move toward a place of satisfaction happens through really understanding that one thing. That's because we all have the tendency to think the worst about ourselves and create limits on what we can imagine ourselves to be. We can't imagine a different possible future if we're mired in beliefs that are informed by old traumas, memories, or self-concepts that are out of date or harmful to us.

Real Conversations to Have with Yourself

When it comes to looking at your own emotional responses to challenges you face, pretend there are no rules.

- What would I really say to someone who hurt me?

- What would I really say to someone whom I admire?

- What would I say to myself about what I need every day to feel comfortable enough to get my work done?

- What is the most intimate thing I'd be comfortable sharing now?

- What is the smallest intimacy I will allow for myself?

You may want to try out some of these ideas in real life—because you actually can. Here's how:

1   **Be real at work and at home.** Give people trust, time, full attention, personalized rewards, and authentic thanks every day. Shift, learn, grow, discover. Allow yourself the freedom to be you. Don't write, don't call, don't video-call, but instead spend time with people in person. Make time to talk with people. When we give time and space to people, we invite them to explore their own ideas out loud with

someone who cares about them. When we give our true attention to people, it becomes easier for them to say what matters to them out loud. It makes sense to give people that honor.

2 **Be accountable and take ownership.** When something goes wrong, or when you don't understand what's at stake or even what's happening, check yourself first. Be proactively transparent about when you're not perfect. It allows others to not be perfect too, so that instead of hiding mistakes, we own up to them and move on.

3 **Build your own self-awareness through these practices every day.** Then challenge yourself to go deeper into why you think the way you do, why you have biases, where your ego makes a choice rather than your heart, your human self. Doing this as a regular practice allows us to let those thoughts go, to get rid of negative intrusions, saving us from ever having those thoughts again.

Fuck the rules.
Be wholly you.

LESSON 10
CELEBRATE EVERYONE

R ESEARCH HAS shown that 40 percent of public companies in North America do not include women on their boards, and many, if not most, Fortune 5000 firms do not consider ethnic diversity an aim despite really obvious changing social values.

The problem with this isn't just that it's unethical or, let's face it, ridiculous. It's that a lack of equity is poor business practice. In fact, it's just plain stupid not to include everyone.

Cold, Hard Facts

Although many companies do not prioritize diversity,[1] according to research:

- A company with a diverse board including women and people of color will result in better ethical performance, meaning that its leaders and senior employees are more likely to follow government regulations, and less likely to commit indirect financial reporting mistakes and engage in less overt fraud.[2]

- A company with a diverse board will be likely to make more money. That's because companies with gender-diverse boards are more likely to innovate, create original patents, and engage in new product development, increasing financial success for a company over both the short and the long term.[3]

- A company with a diverse board results in increased attention to a diverse market and a range of consumer needs, and accuracy in predicting those needs well into the future.[4]

These are cold, hard facts. So there's really no downside to diversity. And there's a hell of a lot of upside.

---

1   Helena Isidro and Márcia Sobral, "The Effects of Women on Corporate Boards on Firm Value, Financial Performance, and Ethical and Social Compliance," *Journal of Business Ethics* 132, no. 1 (2015): 1–19.

2   Cordelia Fine, Victor Sojo, and Holly Lawford-Smith, "Why Does Workplace Gender Diversity Matter? Justice, Organizational Benefits, and Policy," *Social Issues and Policy Review* 14, no. 1 (2020): 36–72; Aida Sijamic Wahid, "The Effects and the Mechanisms of Board Gender Diversity: Evidence from Financial Manipulation," *Journal of Business Ethics* 159 (2019): 705–25.

3   Muhammad Atif, Benjamin Liu, and Allen Huang, "Does Board Gender Diversity Affect Corporate Cash Holdings?" *Journal of Business Finance & Accounting* 46, nos. 7–8 (2019): 1003–29.

4   Dale Griffin, Kai Li, and Ting Xu, "Board Gender Diversity and Corporate Innovation: International Evidence," *Journal of Financial and Quantitative Analysis* 56, no. 1 (2021): 123–54.

If you want an increase in ethical, financial, and legal success, hire people from every background around. Put them on your boards, and, founders, seek out mentors from every possible identity group.

Companies need to be proactive in breaking down these social barriers and allowing for shifts to the status quo for many reasons now commonly discussed today in regard to equity, equality, and inclusion. But one other simple reason companies should focus on diversity and inclusion is so that their financial goals can be achieved. Institutionalizing an expectation of diversity in the work we do should be something we expect, not something we have to be constantly striving for. But this call to action should make sense even without me over-explaining it.

Everyone buys stuff—not just tall white dudes like me. And everyone should be able to buy stuff and follow their own passions and start businesses: I want everyone to have that shot in life. But here are a few practical business questions to think about: Why would a company *not* want to be super-inclusive so they had the potential to sell their products to *all the people*? Why would a company *not* want to build a community that appeals to *all the people* over the longest period of time? Why would the majority of business decision-makers be men when women make more purchasing decisions across every geographic and demographic group? Who understands the lives of average consumers and what they need more: rich elites or people on a payroll?

We should be celebrating more women and more diverse hires of all kinds in business and on boards every day. The real way to straighten out the board equality gap, for example, is for leading companies to flip the table—the boardroom table that is—to a female majority.

Why would a company *not* want to build a community that **appeals to *all the people* over the longest period of time?**

Let's invite everyone in. The table should be open to everyone who understands and values our products—they represent not only the broader spectrum of consumers but also the creativity and diversity of perspectives.

Don't ask yourself why. Ask yourself why not.

Who's with me?

Let's make sure that absolutely anything is possible.

"I don't remember if these words are based on advice that I've been given, but they are the words I passionately believe in," Jan Hall, CEO of M2 Ingredients, began. "Those words are 'anything is possible.' I totally adore mushrooms. I eat them every single day. And in the UK, where I'm from, there's a high incidence of consumption per capita. I had no idea that there was a mushroom-growing company in Carlsbad, like, right in my backyard. Who knew? So it was really a revelation to discover that I'd be interviewing for Om Mushrooms."

Om Mushrooms, a subsidiary of M2 Ingredients, was the first business in which I took a role after I left Manitoba Harvest. Literally a week after stepping out of my founding business, I was an outside chair at Om, acting as interim CEO during the four months before we hired the CEO. And I loved mentoring and working with Jan.

Like hemp, mushrooms are another wonderful gift from Mother Nature that have crossed over from food to supplement to medicine to drug, and they have also been very misunderstood. People understand white button mushrooms. They *think* they understand so-called magic mushrooms and getting high. But we're only just starting to develop psychedelic medicine and the functional uses of mushrooms, especially those linked to psilocybin.

This work is vitally important in several different ways. Psilocybin-assisted psychotherapy could provide needed options for debilitating mental health disorders including PTSD, major depressive disorder, alcohol-use disorder, anorexia nervosa, and more that kill thousands of people every year. But the work Om is doing is also important because of the need for innovation in how we use life-giving plants to help us move toward a more healthy and sustainable human future. And this is where Jan and her commitment to equity come in. Jan brings an impressive background spanning the food, beverage, dietary supplement, consumer health, and skin care categories to her role as CEO. A seasoned hands-on leader with more than thirty years of experience, Jan is responsible for managing all operations and strategic growth, including leading business expansion, brand-building initiatives, and spearheading innovation.

The truth is, Jan was headed for a very mundane and gendered career. In the UK, Jan's mother was a personal assistant for the head of a local agricultural company and her father was a high school teacher, both female-dominated professions. Jan's future was supposed to revolve around her role as a mother, not the other way around. But fate changed the way she saw herself and her value and purpose.

"When my father died when I was eighteen, I needed to work to help my family, and so I had to take up a job in a department store," she told me. "I found that I worked well in business, and so when I could go back to university, I decided to use my degree to go into business rather than teaching, like my mother wanted for me. But even in business, I found myself moving toward working in ways that benefit people. That's really what I truly believe is amazing. That's why I'm here in this company."

However, the fact that she was female remained a difficulty for Jan. "When I worked in particularly large companies," she explained, "it was always a man's world, and often I would be the only woman in the room. And that was really hard. I missed out on promotions, perhaps because I tended to be calm. I wasn't the kind of person to talk over people. I remember one time I was one of three candidates, and I was overlooked despite the fact that I had the most relevant skill set and experience. When that happened, I went to the person who made that decision and actually had it out with him, and soon after, he became one of my biggest supporters."

The fact that Jan ever had to contend with the kind of discrimination that prevented her from taking steps forward in her career is baffling to me. Jan is an outstanding CEO who has the experience and skills to make a huge impact in the natural foods industry.

In order to get out of that mindset of inferiority, Jan now mentors young people, helping them set aside imposter syndrome and focus on what matters to them. What matters to her, she told me, is how she was able to see herself in the role of CEO, and how she could imagine her own future-oriented vision for consumers, society, and her fellow employees into being.

"I believe in what I do, in the power of mushrooms for the Western diet, and if I can go on helping people discover that, that's wild," Jan said. "Our vision is to make a positive difference to people's everyday health through the power of mushrooms. So, we're on a mission to help change the health and wellness of the world, and I am so thrilled to be doing this work. But every bit as important to the work are the people we sit across the table from. I want to work with decent human beings with strong values in life."

Jan is right. And other CEOs agree.

Dror Balshine of Sol Cuisine, one of North America's largest plant-based retail and restaurant product companies, has a similar approach.

"I don't think there's any secret sauce for creating great products that people want to line up for in droves, except for two things," he said to me. "First, emphasize the product.

Choose the better sunflower oil. Don't always look for the cheapest thing out there. Deliver on quality. That's what gets people to click over and over. You can make incremental investments in your product, and take it slow. Second, there's that saying that if you're the smartest person in the room, you're in the wrong room. I always make sure that I'm in a room full of people who are intelligent and whom I can trust. In fact, there are a lot of specific skills required to put a team together, and that's what's made me successful."

There's a shift that's happening in the world when it comes to discovering who we want to be in the future.

The COVID-19 pandemic has given us all an opportunity to break old patterns, and we're seeing this play out in the Great Resignation. The need for a renewed people-centric purpose in business has never been more profound.

Companies do not have to take on an either/or approach, where leaders prioritize only profits or only people. In fact, we know that when companies do not recognize the value of human resources as a primary asset, profits will be negatively affected. We have to act in a way that respects the social reality around us, rather than assuming, as many legacy businesses have in the past, that we ought to have absolute power over our employees.

In the very near future, we're going to see a lot of shifting from what we've been used to in our business modeling toward not only more types of products but also more types of businesses.

"In consumer products, we're sharing a lot more now," Margaret Coons from Nuts for Cheese told me. "And plant-based products are going to tend to be more mainstream. We're all trying new foods, we're experimenting with cutting-edge, exciting alternatives. Sure, massive conglomerate corporations lead our supply of food, but now more and more entrepreneurs have really neat ideas that are changing the world and changing the way the market operates. Business is going to continue to differentiate rather than consolidate. We're in here, making it happen, which is awesome for consumers."

It *is* awesome for consumers! Legacy brands have value, but they don't have to offer the only value. Farm-to-table, localized manufacturing, market selling, and nimble, agile business models that take advantage of (rather than create) climate shifts are going to be necessary if we want to feed the world, let alone make money.

What that means in practical terms is that not only do business leaders have to be more aware of their impact on people, but they also have to see them as true stakeholders. This means that a number of questions need to be asked and answered:

- What are the alternatives to legacy hierarchies and inequities in the workplace?

- If employees no longer accept overwork and low pay, how will companies restructure their profit orientation to come to the table with their workforce?

- Who will make decisions if everyone is a stakeholder, and how will those decisions be made?

- What are the most people-centric values that we can create and sustain in the workplace?

- How can businesses remain accountable for their choices?

- If the failure of profit-driven organizations to offer people-centric environments is evident, then how can we work on what matters on a broader scale at the industry level?

- What companies are achieving these goals at the present time, and where are the gaps for other companies?

I can predict that the future is going to be good with supporting changes in the status quo. Businesses need a sense of human consciousness and awareness if they want to build support in the community. I also see the good energy that we're creating when we take action on people-centric ideas. When we start talking about how good the future can be. Whether it's just inspiring people to change or showing how much change is possible, I'm amped up to see what is coming next.

We all need to be celebrated.

My personal fight for equality across culture, race, and ethnic background is definitely tied to my own experiences of discrimination. It's tied to the social barriers that hit me hard over multiple decades of my life. I was an underprivileged, overweight, geeky kid who got bullied and didn't fit in. I was already fighting for my own equality. Later, I wholly signed up for the passion of fighting for the equality of plants, in the form of cannabis. I still have privileges, though. For me, the need for equality for all people and plants emerged from my lived experience, but I do not take the privileges I have lightly.

What I realized is that even though I want to support equity at all times, not every woman, person of color, differently abled person, or person who identifies in the LGBTQ2S+ community is going to be able to get close enough for me to offer them mentorship.

I mentor as diverse a group of mentees as I can, every day. Since I've started mentoring full-time, I've chatted with probably close to a thousand entrepreneurs, and have done dozens of business tune-ups and a handful of strategic planning sessions. I've been physically practicing that to understand the situations that founders are in and how I can really support them.

Good energy is created when we take action on people-centric ideas. **When we start talking about how good the future can be.**

But to help everyone who deserves a hand up for their great ideas and passion—that's impossible. That's why I started something I call "mass mentorship."

What began as an online clubhouse session with Greg Fleishman, who's a longtime natural products industry friend, became a self-serve entrepreneur toolbox at fatafleishman.org. During our recordings, many of our podcast guest founders would offer audience members a form, template, or structure they relied on in their own work. So, we created a self-serve model where anyone can download an employee charter template or a forecasting model or human resource file idea, or whatever they need to fulfill their dreams.

In 2022, we had approximately 10,000 entrepreneurs access that toolbox. Our offering has been written up in *Forbes*, and I hope that means we're reaching everyone wanting to turn their passion into a realistic and successful business.

In addition, on my *Founder to Mentor* podcast, I offer knowledge from successful founders in the natural products industry directly to listeners. I have a conversation with these leaders to bring out some of their best business strategies and mentorship ideas. With a live audience of industry people to ask questions in the background, I'm aiming to make sure that natural products founders continue helping founders, and that mass mentorship is available for free, everywhere.

Every person I meet, I learn from. Every person I meet, I see myself in them.

That's why every chance I have to give someone a hand up, I'm there for them.

What are you going to do to celebrate everyone?

- **Hire more women.** Put them on your boards. Move them out of that human resources box most corporations land them in and into strategy. If they know and understand people, then they should be at the top of your promotion list.

- **Hire for diversity.** Don't even hesitate here for one second. A range of backgrounds on your team equals a range of insights and points of view, which leads to innovation. Let the team reflect the consumer world you want to create for your brand.

- **Hire for values.** Believe in people who are excited and committed but who also think differently from you. Surround yourself with people who share your values but also want to take on the world.

- **Make sure everyone has the tools they need.** When people come from diverse backgrounds, they won't always have learned how to use the same toolbox right from the get-go. Provide everyone with access to not only resources but also your time.

- **Reflect their worth every day.** Acknowledge the beauty and joy in difference, and ask for opinions. Make people feel safe to open up.

- **Be there.** Every chance you have to give someone a hand up, show up.

LESSON 11
LET YOUR CHANGE CHANGE THE WORLD

M Y DAD has a 50-by-100-foot garden that is full of green-houses. Every year, he grows enough tomatoes to make a couple hundred jars of sauce. I don't know if you've ever had homemade tomato sauce, but it's a staple in every Italian kitchen for a reason. Freshly grown tomatoes on the vine are unlike anything you can find in the supermarket—they're so bright and rich and juicy. Those tomatoes are the foundation of many of our most cherished dishes, and when the sauce is freshly cooked and jarred immediately, it tastes like summer all year round.

The only thing we cross our fingers for is that the batch lasts the whole year until the next set of plants is ready to go.

I've adopted a bunch of what my dad has taught me about gardening, about the joy of exploring how tiny tomato seeds grow into plants. They bloom, they fruit, and then they fade. Making sure that we keep some of the seeds for the next generation of food for our family is a given.

In fact, most of my diet is based on my Mediterranean heritage, but for reasons that go beyond culture. There are five so-called Blue Zones in the world, where people commonly live up to a century or longer: Ikaria, Greece; Okinawa, Japan; Loma Linda, California; Nicoya Peninsula, Costa Rica; and the Ogliastra region of Sardinia, which is an island in my dad's native Italy. Residents eat a lot of seafood, as well as locally grown legumes like soy, fava beans, and chickpeas. Sugar is taboo, and they drink a lot of water. Their staple foods are drawn from what is provided by the water and land, especially in places like Ikaria and Ogliastra, where it is too rocky to grow agricultural crops. Author Dan Buettner reports in his book *The Blue Zones Solution* that their water in particular is known to be calcium- and magnesium-rich, which wards off heart disease and promotes strong bones.

People who live in Blue Zones are generally healthier, but they are also happy. What the world's longest-lived people have that others do not are routines to shed negative stress. Okinawans take a few moments each day to remember their ancestors, Ikarians take a nap, and Sardinians do happy hour. Successful centenarians in the Blue Zones put their families first. This means keeping aging parents and grandparents nearby or in the home, lowering disease and mortality rates of children. They invest in their children with time and love.

Anyone can follow these patterns of eating, drinking enough good water, resting, and supporting their families, but the research data showed something else important: these habits were generational. They were hardwired into the social structure of these villages. In places like Okinawa, where lifestyles were changing and families were acting differently than they had in the past, the results in terms of longevity also changed.

What people intrinsically know and what they do automatically without question is what matters. When we know, we know. And when we don't, we fail to take life up on what it can offer us.

It's crazy, you know. Every house had a garden until around the '50s and '60s, when societal norms started to change. People became mesmerized by industrial food systems. All of a sudden, they thought they no longer needed a garden because they could buy all of that food at the grocery store. Instead of gardens, families cultivated perfectly mowed grass out front, thinking that they'd look more successful. The whole "keeping up with the Joneses" performance everyone was putting on in their front yard required them to seem as if they were above the manual labor of seeding, plotting, and growing.

And we're not over it yet. Don't get me wrong: the interest in natural and organic foods and clean eating has grown in recent years. But the needle has moved from around 5 percent of the food supply maybe twenty years ago to only between 10 and 15 percent right now. That means that the majority of our food supply is still significantly poisoned by chemicals and additives our bodies don't know what to do with. Added to that is the fact that in North America, one-third of the food that leaves farms is currently wasted or thrown away. And global water shortages mean that there's less water for agriculture, which may lead to shortages in the food supply in vulnerable areas of the world over the long term.

We're not helping ourselves by forgetting what actually fuels our bodies and how to grow it. There was a sudden shift in awareness during the COVID-19 pandemic's first year, especially, when people started to realize the value of growing their own food. In some cities, people began to test the waters. There were kitchen gardens on front lawns again and shared vegetable gardens on suburban streets.

It's small changes like that, even in the panic of food supply chain issues, that can show us again how simply we can shift toward a new way of thinking about how we feed ourselves and our families.

We have to become more comfortable with changing who we are and living up to our highest selves.

Change, as we know, is a constant. But so is our fear of change.
We are constantly faced with new information, new ideas and leaps in technologies, changing environmental and economic

We have to become more comfortable with changing **who we are and living up to our highest selves.**

priorities, and opportunities that arise in front of us. We have to learn constantly, whether we like it or not. We also manage expected changes, such as those of the seasons and the aging of our parents and our children. The media we watch changes as Netflix shows rise and fall in popularity. The toothpaste that we used to use tastes different when we discover new, healthier ingredients.

Often, these legacy patterns extend to our personalities and the lived experiences we have. Genetic memory, the collective ideas of the other people we spend time with, personal habits, what was taught to us as children—all of these aspects of life become repeated and ingrained. The problem is that we live on a kind of neurological autopilot, which is both a good thing and a challenging one. These autonomous processes are running in the background, helping us navigate the repetitive parts of life like driving a car, making phone calls, and picking up groceries we love to eat. Our familiar choices are made over and over again, and they become legacy patterns.

Some legacy patterns are great, like Dad's tomatoes. It's ingrained in me, based on my family and culture, to at least try to keep on growing and cooking these fruits.

Other legacy patterns aren't healthy for us or the world around us. We can't seem to shake industrial agriculture, and we make it hard for small farms to succeed because we want to pay less every day.

We've gotten used to an economy where we want more, rather than better. But we can entirely change the way we approach things. Nowadays, consumers vote with their dollars and support changes brought on by businesses doing the "right" thing.

The natural products industry is working more symbiotically with what our new understanding of our needs has taught us. We know our environment is worth saving.

"Environmental health" refers to how we manage environmental factors that may adversely impact human health. "Ecological health," however, is the understanding that the ecological environment forms the basis of all healthy life on this planet. Ecological health provides people not only with air, food, and water but also with many goods and services that have the potential to increase human health and well-being.

Consumers gaining greater interest in health has resulted in the creation of healthier packaged foods, more supplements, and a nutrition focus. We better understand the role of organics and clean eating, and how allergens work. We have created a level of awareness in which the natural products industry has become very mainstream.

The good news, therefore, is that with this growth in awareness, even though we are on autopilot, newer entrepreneurs can come in big.

- Founders of natural foods companies can offer breakthrough options for consumers who are interested in health.

- They can easily differentiate themselves, put a truly novel product on supermarket shelves, and then break through the rest of the noise.

- They can work together with their nation to move their natural foods from niche-only at the health food store to every grocery store.

Our understanding of how food can and should work has meant that we are taking up a larger and larger portion of the food supply, and despite the fact that we are fighting Big Food, we're winning.

New information has to mean innovation.

While I would like to see gardens in every front yard, I also know that connecting with our homegrown ability to keep us healthy is going to remain an area of concern as the world's population grows. We have to support founders who get to the heart of what we all need—to access organic food anywhere and everywhere.

The entrepreneurial way of doing things is that if we can't agree on what needs to be done first, we should *just start doing things.*

Food care is self-care, and our food comes from farming. We have to start with understanding our true relationship with the food we eat and how we can't separate ourselves from it.

Sometimes, we need to move beyond our nation to our world. And Dror Balshine from Sol Cuisine has worked very hard to change our world.

"Back in the nineties, fast food was all about flipping burgers," he said to me. "Sure, there were a few vegan restaurants around, but if you wanted to grab something to eat for lunch, you'd try to find a restaurant like Subway and basically have a sandwich with lettuce and tomato without dressing on it. Basically, I saw that you couldn't get much of anything that was, you know, more than french fries. So to fill that need, Sol Cuisine was creating a brand that would be sold in food retailers and started doing business with fast food chains."

Like Manitoba Harvest, Sol Cuisine is considered, in some ways, to be a legacy brand, and Dror is one of the earliest plant-based product entrepreneurs in North America. He's one of the people who really defined that category way before it was cool to be vegan. That's why Dror has literally taken his product door-to-door across this continent. He's been knocking on doors and offering up his amazing cauliflower wings and vegan bites to people who've never tried plant-based meats before. He's been telling his own story to families and asking them to share a meal with him, right on their front porches.

Sitting down and talking to people is why Dror is revered in this industry. It's not just about giving out samples and selling a good product, even though Dror is amazing at that. It's about the chance to build that capacity to see what we talk about when we open the door to something new. We can learn what we value now and what excites us about the future. He's out there asking questions so he can actually understand consumers' answers, but he's also sharing his own story. So even if he is a legacy entrepreneur, Dror is open to whatever is behind the next door.

Change changes us, so be the change. We never know what we're going to face tomorrow, but we know things are going to keep changing, and we know that we're going to need each other. Living in a Blue Zone or not, we know that self-care includes taking care of our ecosystems and revisiting old ways of thinking about food while being open to new visions for our future.

I've never had an issue with change, which has served me well. Change represents the full circle of who we are, so much so that acknowledging that is almost spiritual to me. I always think the future is going to be better than I expect, and maybe that's because my own personal growth and change through business allowed me to see new ways of adopting ideas, and I've fully embodied that be-the-change philosophy.

We can all naturally, intuitively make a choice to create something when we notice what's missing. Just like the old game of "keeping up with the Joneses," though, we all have a tendency to see some things but not others. We might see something that is shiny or bold over something that is subtle but very important. We might see something that demands

Change changes us, **so be the change.**

our attention over something that is simply there around every corner, over and over again. We might see what we want to see, rather than something that we ought to see.

Instead of leaning back on old paradigms in business and life, if we're going to build outward and solve big, entrenched problems, we need to do things in a completely different way, and draw on our emotional awareness skills.

- We need to become clear about knowing when it's time to do the work and recognizing if it is even our work to do.

- We need to trust ourselves to notice all the things that matter to others and to us, and be a witness to known problems so that we can become part of collective solutions, adding to what's already been achieved.

- We need to build consciousness and awareness and support of global issues in the community.

- We need to bring good energy to the table. I feel more inspired talking about how good the future can be and more energized by inspiring change in others than dwelling on problems we didn't create.

Together, we will change the world. The more we help the community around us, the more millions of lives we will impact. It is possible to build a sustainable, health-giving, and kind business that is also financially successful. If I can do it, anyone can.

Or grow tomatoes.

Either way, it's a good thing.

LESSON 12
LIVE YOUR PRACTICE

DIDN'T MENTION this before, but I played professional pool when I was young, from the time I was fourteen until I was twenty-two. In fact, I played tournament pool up to six nights a week across town. After dropping out of school, pool provided me with a purpose, one that allowed me to build a rather unique set of skills for someone so young. Hustle. Geometry. Concentration. Flow.

Pool is a very technical game. To be good, you need to understand all of its mechanics: how you hold the cue, how you position it, how the ball geometry works, how you hit one ball into one pocket or another one.

Then you have to know the sequencing of the game as a whole. You need to shoot the balls out into the right positions so you're able to run balls on the table in the right order.

But what I found out early on is that if you're thinking about the game while you're playing it, you're never going to be good. You have to get into a flow state, where you've trained your mind to do what it has to without thinking out all the steps. You understand the technicality of the game, but your brain's not trying to work it all out ahead of time. Instead, you're just actioning it naturally.

When the business started to get too busy and I couldn't play every day, I missed it. I started exploring different triggers to get myself back into that flow state. Of course, exercise became one of my key triggers. Like a runner's high, exercise creates that flow state for me. So does listening to certain music for certain tasks, whether it's a workout or I'm trying to be creative or solve a problem.

Flow is a real thing. It's not just about me, and it actually applies to business. Flow is a mental state of functioning in which a person is completely immersed in a sense of energy, focus, full engagement, and enjoyment of the creative process.

As explored by researcher Mihaly Csikszentmihalyi, flow is the creative process that can be triggered by trying to answer a problem that has no direct solution. It's a bit like a subconscious force that brings hidden thoughts and ideas to the surface because we don't actually know what to do. Flow can result in an immediate creative response, which Csikszentmihalyi suggests is the merging of action and awareness. At the same time, flow cannot be achieved without knowing which different paths can be taken to reach the same end goal. Practicing flow, therefore, is a way of training the brain to look at all of the possibilities that are open to us.

And flow *is* inherently similar to a game—with diverse, flexible, and appropriate challenges; clear goals; and a self-reflective capacity. A flow experience can include fun *and* action. It can also help us feel like we're realizing our own potential and our ability to explore spontaneous trial and error.

We may not realize the power of a single breath.

Kriya yoga has become my new flow practice. It includes pretty easy-to-try breathwork and meditation exercises, and anyone can do it. Because it's a part of my everyday life, now I can take a breath or two and use that as a trigger to get into that flow state. I can use minor touch meditations, like rubbing two fingers together, and really be mindful about what I'm doing. I'm not worrying about the future or the past. I'm very much in the moment and doing my best at whatever I'm doing.

I'm not saying you have to follow my vibe. You can play pool if you want to. But I've found that the more time I'm in a state of flow, the happier I am in life, and the closer I am to making my best day ever.

I gave every breath I had to my business, and it gave everything to me.

But—and this is a very important thing to recognize—the reason that was the case was not that I powered through everything till I was overworked and burned out. The reason my business and I have had a reciprocal, mutually supportive relationship is that we found a way to grow in sync with one another.

The very definition of being alive is being *in* growth. All the time. Everything in our lives, in our experience of life as we emerge, as we mature, and as we explore what we want to do and who we want to be, pushes us to grow. At times, it seems like an evolutionary imperative. We grow or we die— or perhaps it's more like we grow *until* we die. We have no other choice.

What I do know, however, is that the term "personal growth" is loaded. And that's probably the case because the more we work on our personal growth, the closer we get to living in true integrity. I've talked about integrity a lot in this book. Your integrity is important because it's at the heart of building goodwill with your community and creating a strong brand, but it actually means something to us as individuals too. Integrity, or a lack of it, can define us. If you don't have it, people know. They just do. And that's going to affect your entire life.

Living in integrity with ourselves can feel difficult to begin with. Pointing at, and living through, the highest integrity version of ourselves is the highest meditation of life.

There's a scale to it.

The very definition of being alive **is being *in* growth.**

We know, in our bones, what living in integrity is. I actually don't have to define it for you. You already know. But let's be honest: things, people, and life . . . all of it gets in the way.

- We know that our bodies would feel better, for example, if we ate organically, but when the workday is over, sometimes the easiest thing to do is get takeout and sit in front of the television.

- We know that we would have more clarity throughout the day if we just put down our phones and talked to one another in kind, soft tones, but we're often called to the next meeting quickly and we have to review emails from three people before we arrive.

- We know that we'd be able to rest better if we had a long bath with Epsom salts before bed, but often we are too tired to do anything except tumble under the covers and close our eyes, only to toss and turn a few hours later.

But the fundamental integrity we can build with our highest self . . . well, that's a different story. If you're aspiring to have a high-integrity relationship with yourself, you have to walk in high compassion with yourself. That's the part that, when you think about it, seems like it's an unobtainable goal. It's because it's hard to imagine ourselves living a really wonderful life. It's easier to imagine ourselves falling asleep on that takeout night than it is to imagine what our lives might look like if we really moved toward integrity. That's why we don't strive for it. We stop trying.

The unrelenting pressure of setting aside our integrity is there, however, everywhere we look. Which people around you are lauded and valued as successes? Think about it for a second. Which people are presented to you as heroes?

Businesspeople? Politicians? Nobel Prize winners? Marvel Universe superheroes? Sometimes it feels as if we have very little in common with these folks, and, if you think deeply, some of these people may not have treated others well in order to achieve their goals personally. Some of them aren't *actually real people.* Yet, we have externally edified the definition of success that requires us to be absolutely powerful heroes, and look down on integrity as a weakness. We don't place a significant value on having a high quality of life if it doesn't come with the trappings of wealth, power, and social position that we've put on a pedestal. This means that we've created a semiconscious agreement that to be living in high integrity is to be foolish, because someone will take advantage of you.

But here's a secret. Believing that we are foolish for doing the right thing in life is a way of justifying our behaviors so we feel less bad about living outside of integrity.

We need to give life to what we focus on and keep the good vibes flowing daily. If we're out of touch with what is actually right for us, we're going to lose that ability to keep in flow.

The trick to any success is to finish what you start, no matter what.

So how do we get to the finish line?

We've got to get everything out of the way. In fact, we really have to get mindful of the choices we're making. But a lot of us tell ourselves that it isn't actually possible for us to be successful. And I'm here to tell you that's not true. It really isn't. The reason you might be feeling scared, or as if you don't have what it takes, is that imposter syndrome I keep talking about.

If you can clear your own path, you'll be able to look at things a lot differently. There are a few fundamental questions you can ask yourself to clear your mind so that you can start exploring your path to a flow state and discover the right state of mind to follow your passion without anything getting in the way.

Think about these questions in order:

1 **What do I think is stopping me from success?** Think about absolutely anything you feel is in your way today. It can include any challenges that just don't feel good or make you feel less confident, less like you. Maybe these things feel too big to tackle in one go. It can be anything that's bothering you: your health, the fact that you haven't paid your taxes, your workload.

2 **What do I think I should be doing about it?** Think about the solution most people would normally apply to this problem. Write it down. Is it something like filling in all the forms to file your taxes? Doing extra work on the weekend? Getting into that habit of working out by forcing yourself to get up at five in the morning?

3 **Why do I feel like I can't do the normal thing to resolve my issue?** What's the reason you're telling yourself there's a barrier you have to leap before you get there?

4 **What is actually true about what I'm telling myself?** What if the reason is something as simple as "I haven't done this before and I'm nervous"? Or, "I want to take an unconventional path"?
   Remember that there's an alternative way forward.

We have to trust ourselves to be just our own best *us*.

Very few of us come into this world with the hardwired skill of knowing how to choose a path of purpose.

And, let's be honest, a lot of us are tired. Many of us live disconnected from our passion, and the only way to get there, to connect or reconnect, is to try. But personal growth is a phrase, and a phase, that doesn't let us rest. We could do nothing and stop striving. But we're all here to answer the same questions: What is a good life? What is a life *well lived*? What are we all aiming for? What is a working life that really *works*?

Over the course of my life, I have become much more aware of the fact that there isn't anyone who will come along to hand us the key to the kingdom. We won't necessarily feel fulfilled when we get an education, find the perfect job, get married, or even attain our highest fantasy of founding a company or building a community or nation.

In fact, getting to where we want to go is our own challenge, alone. There is no road to discover our best self that we can't define for ourselves, right now. There is no special trick.

But before we get there, I have to say that one of the most important things I've learned along my own path is that we all have to have compassion for ourselves. That means that trusting ourselves can take time.

A four-year-old child who doesn't want to give up the Xbox controller maybe isn't confident that she'll get the controller back again, so she acts out and gets emotional. We can totally see where she's coming from. We forgive her because she hasn't learned the ropes yet, nor would we expect her to have. In a similar way, if you're replaying that last bad meeting in your head a thousand times, then you may be living in a context where you haven't quite figured out how to navigate working with a certain personality type, or you may not have had the resources at hand that you needed to solve a problem for a client. That's not a bad thing—it's just a thing you haven't mastered yet. You're okay. You can have compassion for yourself that you're still learning your way. You can still trust yourself to figure it out eventually.

If we don't trust ourselves to finish what we set out to do, it will never happen. We have to support a life of experimentation, reflection, and creativity so we can see the opportunities we already have in front of us every day. We're allowed to give ourselves the space to be curious about what matters, what makes us passionate, and trust that it's all going to work out.

Because it will work out.

We just have to show up. We just have to live fully and in flow and in integrity, and let growth happen in alignment with who we really are as people.

We just have to try to have our best day ever.

CONCLUSION
YOU ARE
UNSTOPPABLE

IMAGINE, FOR a moment, that you are unstoppable.

Imagine the whole-you version of yourself, capable of conceptualizing your brilliant future and living your best day ever, every day. What does it feel like to be that person, starting every day fulfilling your own needs, filling your own cup so you have enough momentum, energy, and joy to share with everyone around you? What could it mean to build a financially viable, sustainable, health-giving, and kind business?

It feels great. It *is* great to get to know yourself well enough, to build a community around you strong enough, and to create a business vision inclusive enough that you know you don't have to stop for anything.

And that's why I want you to remember the beginning of my story.

- I, Mike Fata, have been very scared, lonely, and disconnected from my own needs.

- I've taken an unconventional path in life, from the time I was in elementary school, because I've faced some difficult challenges.

- I've been afraid of seeing myself as successful.

- I didn't start out with money or fame; I started out hobbled by childhood trauma, physical pain, and no formal education.

- I have become very successful, but I've done this by making my own life better first, one step at a time.

- I didn't push myself to succeed at the expense of my mental and physical health; I built up my self-care and care for my business in parallel.

If I can do these things, and get the help of all the mentors I have needed along the way, you can also do these things. Just because you grow up without material wealth, or the expected business education, or a body that fits into social ideals of ability or beauty, does not mean you can't create the life you imagine for yourself.

Unconventional paths do lead to success if you believe in yourself and act on making your best day ever a reality.

Your highest self is always available to you.

I don't mean that you have to aim for perfection. No one expects that. Not at all. But whether we're talking about a business idea, a human resource policy, or what you're going to eat for dinner, you can reach for the best-day, best-you version of what that looks like. Even if you don't get there immediately, you're serving your own needs when you make a choice that feels even 1 percent better.

That's because what I call growth is not a project. There is no formula or plan to follow. There is no right answer to the challenge of knowing yourself and what your best day, your best business, looks like. You don't have to fix yourself, because you are not broken. Personal growth is the process of having an organic, living, adult conversation with ourselves. It is an open-ended conversation that is filled with more questions than we could ever count. We need to ask ourselves questions to help us discover our own story, and not count the gaps between where we are now and where we want to be. The questions we ask ourselves are really the bread crumb trail we can create to get back to who we are, underneath all of the life experiences that have clouded our hopes and dreams.

So think about that for a moment. And then think about the twelve lessons in this book—the lessons that start you off on a path to grow yourself and your life as big as you want:

1   You can mark off a win if you try out a new habit for an hour, and add up those million little wins over a lifetime.

2   You can front-end giving your time and effort to helping others.

3   You can have your best day ever, every day, and you already have the resources to get started.

4   You will not fail if you are really passionate about a project, because you'll do it every day, and you won't accept anything less than amazing.

5   You and your business will benefit deeply from taking the time to connect, communicate, and listen.

6   You are not allowed to believe someone who doesn't believe in you.

7   You can use honesty, integrity, transparency, and a can-do attitude to make decisions that are ethical and achievable.

8   You can remember that if it takes a village to raise a family, it takes a nation to raise an entrepreneur.

9   You are a feeling being who thinks, not a thinking being who feels, and you can honor emotions in business.

10 You can be a part of the shift that's happening in the world, and celebrate everyone.

11 You do not have to fear change.

12 You know that to be alive is to grow.

Living your best day ever, living that highest-self life, comes with listening to, believing in, and giving to yourself first.
It also comes with listening to, believing in, and giving to others. You, your friendships, your communities, and your world are intertwined.

This is how you grow.

And it's not just about having a growth-oriented mindset. That's great—I want you to feel hopeful. But you also have to *do* these things, act on these lessons—not just imagine what is possible—to become truly unstoppable.

What does that look like in practice? Choose one of the lessons and see what it feels like to put it into action, even at that 1 percent better level. You don't have to do the lessons in order. Find the one that feels reachable for you, and then put that 1 percent into play. It may feel a bit uncomfortable to try at first, but the discomfort won't last forever.

Taking on a new aim for yourself is exactly like growing a new muscle. There's a little soreness because you haven't worked on yourself in that way before. But this is where you have to trust this process a bit. Since you're reading this book right now, you're already on that growth trajectory. One win will soon become five, then ten, and then a thousand, and then suddenly you're at that million-win mark. That's because these lessons actually work. They've worked for me, my business, the dozens of people I directly mentor at any given time. And that's why I feel compelled to share my life's work with you.

You cannot ignore your own experiences, traumas, or gifts, because they are assets to becoming who you want to be. As I've said, the world is waking up to the qualities that an unconventional path offers all of us, and that includes every one of us who used to see ourselves as limited, as lesser than, and as different or scared. We need to be increasingly transparent with ourselves, but we also have to accept each other's so-called limitations as the benefits they can be. We will no longer be vulnerable if we create space for everyone to grow into whom they have the potential to be.

In fact, we are all continuously growing. The choice we make is: Into what? How are we shaping our growth? What are we choosing to feed in our bodies, minds, and spirits, and what are we choosing to suffocate? How can we add the right set of ideas, incentives, or values to our personal growth so we can create the environment to be not just successful entrepreneurs but also happy ones? Entrepreneurs who eke out ways to make the world around us that much better?

All of us want to pursue the path that matters to us, so we actually have to start there. We have to give ourselves that opportunity to do something cool. In fact, it shouldn't be a gift; it should be a given that we do what we want to do.

I want to make it as easy as possible for up-and-coming entrepreneurs to be successful. I want to give you open access to what I've done right and where I've failed in the last quarter-century along my personal and business pathway. And we all learn more by sharing our own stories, myself included. I've been where you are, and I know how it feels.

There are no imposters, only growing people almost ready to take their chance.

It doesn't have to be you against the world.

I'm here with you.

And I know you're unstoppable.

Now's your chance to grow.

ACKNOWLEDGMENTS

THANK YOU to everyone who has helped me grow.

The list, of course, starts with my amazing family. They not only put up with my entrepreneurial craziness over the last thirty or so years, but they helped me hone my skills, and they shared the values that guide my work today. My love for community and my compassion for others are a result of the love and care they provided for me every day.

I'd also like to thank my own mentors. John Holtmann, John Anthony, Mark Ragland, and Ryan Black, you've helped show me the way forward. If it were not for you, I would not have had the courage to make hard decisions, hire great people, build an amazing team, and follow my passion. You've given me the tools to pass on what I've learned to the next generation.

My business community keeps me growing. I want to reach out to honor the Young Presidents' Organization (YPO), the Canadian Health Food Association (CHFA), and the Canadian Organic Trade Association (COTA). My mentees, my portfolio companies, and their founders all challenge me every day and keep inspiring me to help, to inspire, and to dream.

And of course, I have to thank Lisa Thomas-Tench and the wonderful publishing team that made this book possible. To everyone at Page Two, you've assisted me as I've watched my ideas grow into a solid mentoring plan, accessible to the world.

Finally, to everyone who's been at my side as I started my business, and as I have moved toward a vocation as a mentor, I thank you. There are too many of you to count, and for your time, commitment, and connection, I am grateful.

FURTHER READING

Buettner, Dan. *The Blue Zones Solution: Eating and Living Like the World's Healthiest People*. Washington, DC: National Geographic Books, 2015.

Csikszentmihalyi, Mihaly. *Flow: The Psychology of Optimal Experience*. New York: Harper Perennial, 2008.

Dweck, Carol. *Mindset: The New Psychology of Success*. New York: Ballantine, 2008.

Erasmus, Udo. *Fats That Heal, Fats That Kill: The Complete Guide to Fats, Oils, Cholesterol and Human Health*. Summertown, TN: Alive Books, 1993.

Greenleaf, Robert K. *The Power of Servant-Leadership*. Oakland, CA: Berrett-Koehler, 1998.

Liker, Jeffrey K. *The Toyota Way: 14 Management Principles from the World's Greatest Manufacturer*. New York: McGraw-Hill, 2004.

ABOUT
THE AUTHOR

INSPIRING PERSONAL and professional growth, Mike Fata cofounded Manitoba Harvest Hemp Foods in 1998, and since that time has become a leader in natural health, nutrition, hemp foods, organic agriculture, sustainable business, and entrepreneurship. Mike is the host of the *Founder to Mentor* podcast, lifetime member (past chairman) of the Canadian Health Food Association (CHFA), lifetime member (past chairman) of the Young Presidents' Organization (YPO Manitoba), and investor/advisor to a portfolio of companies. After multiple nine-figure exits in his industry, Mike now coaches and mentors natural products entrepreneurs, helping them discover their authentic business passions and live their best lives every day.

BRIAN RUDOLF

Keep On Growing

Finding a mentor isn't about finding someone to help you. It's about learning about yourself, building awareness about what you need and want, and showing up to places where you're going to get access to skill-building. Sometimes that feels like a lot, so I wanted to let you know I'm here to help.

Listen to my podcast.

The *Founder to Mentor* podcast connects you with world-class founder mentors to inspire your personal and professional growth. Join me to explore key insights from my experience as an entrepreneur, an investor, and a mentor helping entrepreneurs to succeed in the business world. Connect to your favorite platform here: **mikefata.ca/podcast**.

Access free entrepreneurial tools.

At Fata & Fleishman Mentorship (**fatafleishman.org**), you can access and download free resources I've developed with fellow mentor Greg Fleishman. We help you get started on your path to entrepreneurship, develop a clear strategy for your business, and accelerate your growth.

Get my newsletter.

If you've liked what you've read here, you'll love getting my follow-up lessons in your inbox. At **mikefata.ca/newsletter**, you can sign up for my newsletter The Unstoppable Entrepreneur and get inspiring and actionable advice to become unstoppable.

Invite me to speak.

Onstage, I lead from my heart and inspire the next generation of entrepreneurs. I bring audiences along on a journey to help them discover their authentic business passions and live their best lives every day. To book me for a speaking engagement, go to **mikefata.ca/speaking**.

Tell me what you think.

I'd love to hear what you've learned about your own entrepreneurial vision from reading *Grow*. And if you think this book might help others, drop me a positive review on your favorite online retailer's website or reading community. It would really help get the word out.

Connect with me every day.

Don't stop asking questions. Give yourself permission to step right into a conversation with me. I'm online where you're at, and I'm open to hearing about your big idea.

 @themikefata

Made in the USA
Las Vegas, NV
16 August 2024